Evaluating Students

*How teachers justify and defend their marks
to parents, students, and principals*

Alex Shirran

Pembroke Publishers Limited

Dedication:
For lovely Miki, and all aspirants like her.

© 2006 Pembroke Publishers
538 Hood Road
Markham, Ontario, Canada L3R 3K9
www.pembrokepublishers.com

Distributed in the U.S. by Stenhouse Publishers
480 Congress Street
Portland, ME 04101-3400
www.stenhouse.com

We acknowledge the financial support of the Government of Canada through the Book Publishing Industry Development Program (BPIDP) for our publishing activities.

We acknowledge the assistance of the OMDC Book Fund, an initiative of the Ontario Media Development Corporation.

Library and Archives Canada Cataloguing in Publication

Shirran, Alex
    Evaluating students: how teachers justify and defend their marks to parents, students, and principals / Alex Shirran.

Includes index.
ISBN 13: 978-1-55138-206-7
ISBN 10: 1-55138-206-7

    1. Grading and marking (Students) I. Title.

LB3051.S55 2006   371.27'2   C2006-902677-7

Editor: Kat Mototsune
Cover design: John Zehethofer
Typesetting: Jay Tee Graphics

Printed and bound in Canada
9 8 7 6 5 4 3 2 1

Contents

Introduction

"Everyone thinks they are experts when it comes to teaching... after all, everyone has gone to school."

The most perceptive comment I have heard regarding the profession of teaching came from one of my professors during my undergraduate studies at university. She remarked, "Everyone thinks they are experts when it comes to teaching... after all, everyone has gone to school." During my years of dealing with parents and students in the public schools, this observation has been reaffirmed in my mind time and time again. The reality is that, for most adults, their knowledge, perceptions, and beliefs about teaching are the products of childhood memories and impressions. Children—and parents—are blissfully unaware of the subtle and unobtrusive instructional strategies employed by teachers, the extensive instructional and curricular planning that occurs, the testing and implementation of new programs, the psychological profiling of students, the multidisciplinary meetings regarding students, and the backroom politics of staffing. Yet, despite this unfamiliarity with pedagogy, everyone with a child seems to think that he or she knows best how to teach and to evaluate students in a classroom setting.

Marks and letter grades are not simply assigned. Rather, teachers evaluate students and justify those evaluations using sound, recognized, and accepted educational practices. The typical teacher will have attended a teacher-education program at a college or university for several years where he or she learned "the rules of teaching"— *how* to teach and *how* to evaluate students. Good teaching and evaluation are based on years of data-driven research findings and, for this reason, all teachers in all teacher-education programs learn the same teaching methods and practices, which they are then required to use in their classrooms. At least, this is true in theory. The simple reality is that the evaluation of other people's children is a great deal more political than is divulged in the teacher-training courses of the universities. Indeed, at no time in the past have parents and students been so capable of holding teachers accountable for their educational decisions and judgments as they can today. The almost obsessive concern regarding marks shown by many parents and students has created the need for professional teachers to be well-versed in the theory, practice, and politics of marking, and to be able to justify and defend their evaluation and teaching practices, lest their professional reputations be thrown into question.

Recently, I saw an interview with a children's advocate who had used letter grades to rate children's perceptions of their parents' child-rearing practices. When the interviewer asked how the letter grades were determined, she stammered, "Oh, you know, like what they do in school. We just assigned letter grades based on how well the parents did." And there it was, the idea that evaluation is a natural, if not haphazard, consequence of schooling.

Both the experienced and the beginning teacher can learn from the evaluation mistakes and foibles of other teachers; metaphorically speaking, one should not have to touch the stove to discover if it will burn. To this end, each chapter analyzes case studies in which a teacher faces some evaluation dilemma or has made some error in marking judgment. Also, specific strategies are presented that the teacher can use in his or her classroom and school setting to prevent complaints from occurring, to rectify them when they do occur, and to strengthen current evaluation practices.

This book, through the use of real-life case studies, shows teachers how to avoid the pitfalls and problems commonly associated with marking student work and assigning grades.

The Three Conditions of Marking

The Well-Intentioned Teacher

Several days after returning her students' graded papers, an English teacher was approached by the parents of one of her students. They demanded that the teacher justify the mark given, and also raise the mark awarded. Dissatisfied with the teacher's reasoning and response, they filed a complaint with the school principal, who investigated the matter. The principal noted in his report that, during an informal interview with the teacher, it became apparent that standard evaluation procedures were not being used and that this teacher's only defence seemed to be, "I have been teaching for over 25 years now. I know the difference between an A paper and a C+ paper." The principal concluded that, while the teacher's assignments were engaging and did address the required course goals, the teacher's evaluation methods were flawed, inaccurate, and invalid.

The teacher in this first case likely had the best of intentions when evaluating her students. Unfortunately, by failing to recognize and follow basic requirements in the evaluation process, she put her professional reputation in jeopardy and gave cause for concern among parents, students, and school administrators. Yes, teachers, due to their professional experiences and training, seem to know intuitively what an A paper looks like; however, the same can not be said for students and their parents. Too often, students do not receive the marks they believe they are entitled to on assignments and tests simply because they do not know how the teacher evaluates and what the teacher requires. In order to minimize the potential for communication problems and conflict, all teachers working in the public education system must articulate clearly and specifically to their students how they will mark student work. This means that, prior to writing any assignment, students must be informed of the teacher's expectations. While this sounds simple enough, even experienced teachers at times fail to address all aspects of the marking process, thereby leaving themselves open to censure and criticism.

Before any student begins working on any assignment for any class, the teacher must clearly and publicly state the three components of evaluation:

1. a stated *criteria level*
2. the *academic level of thought*
3. a *statement of conditions*

Teachers must be clear about this point: every school in every school district requires that these three parts of the marking process be clearly stated to the students and parents for any given assignment. A teacher who does not state these three components may inadvertently put himself or herself in professional jeop-

> Teachers, due to their professional experiences and training, seem intuitively to know what an A paper looks like; however, the same can not be said for students and their parents.

ardy, and his or her students at academic risk. At this point, the three components of the marking process need to be examined more closely.

1. Marking Criteria

Report-card letter grades seem to have an almost mystical quality for parents and students—no one is fully sure what they mean or how they were derived, only that they are in some way important. Some parents keep their child's report cards for years, occasionally bringing them out from storage and sharing them with the child, as if to say, "See, this is who you once were." And yet, what do report-card letter grades really mean? What is the difference between an A and a B+? How do teachers determine which assignments deserve an A and which ones deserve a B, or even a C? These sound like simple questions that should be easy to answer. But they are not. Students and parents frequently think of an A as meaning *excellent*, a B as *very good*, and a C as *average*. Likewise, grades are often interpreted as representing a percent (for example, A = 90%, B = 75%, C+ = 65%, and so on). However, what does *excellent* (or 90%) mean, and how did the teacher arrive at that score for a student?

> The standards of academic performance or proficiency required by a student to receive a specific letter grade are referred to as the *criteria*.

The degree or amount of academic performance or proficiency required by a student to receive a specific letter grade is referred to as the marking criteria. Criteria levels may be created by individual classroom teachers or by groups of teachers at the departmental level, and clearly specify the features, points, details, and skills that must be exhibited by any student in order to receive a particular letter grade. The teacher must determine in advance of assigning the work the required proficiency levels, and these are often based on the teacher's own personal experiences and expectations. Since the purpose of any assignment is not to try to trick or confuse the students, but to allow the teacher to measure student learning, the criteria must be stated publicly and clearly. For example, here is a simple history question on which students may be expected to write:

> Describe the methods of hunting and gathering used in the Jomon Period of Ancient Japan.

For this question, the teacher may determine a student's mark using the following criteria:

> A (90%) = The student discusses and includes residential stability, stone implements, pottery use, collective burials and cemeteries, the permanence of homes, and shifting residences; and provides two examples for each concept.

> B (75%) = The student discusses residential stability, pottery use, and provides one example for each concept.

> C (60%) = The student discusses pottery use and does not provide any examples.

Increasingly, laypeople are using the jargon of teaching even if they do not fully understand the meaning behind the terms. Teachers will find even very young children precociously asking, "And what is the marking criteria [*sic*] for this assignment?" While such an inquiry should be welcomed by the teacher, it does underscore a failing of some educators. Most teachers, at some time or other, have neglected to articulate their marking criteria to parents and students, and this mistake can have negative consequences for the academic achievement of students and the professional autonomy of the teacher. When we adults are evaluated by other adults, we expect transparency in the evaluation process. When we take a driving test, for example, we know exactly what we must do and not do in order to obtain our licence. When we play a board game or an organized sport, we know the rules we must follow and the behaviors we must exhibit in order to win. So also must students know the rules of the marking game if they are to be successful. Unfortunately, some teachers do not take the time to express their marking criteria simply because criteria do take time to create.

The marking criteria may take the form of a grid called a *marking rubric*. In the Detailed Marking Rubric (see below), each box or cell represents a level of performance that can be matched to a corresponding letter grade. The use of a marking rubric has numerous advantages for teachers: it allows the teacher to mark many assignments quickly and efficiently; it allows the teacher to justify and support the mark given to a student, should the student or parent later complain; it provides marking consistency; it allows students to become better judges of the quality of their work; it is easy to explain to parents and allows parents to see what the child needs to do to increase his grade; it allows the quality of a student's work to fall within several boxes and letter-grade categories, thereby allowing the teacher to assign a separate value to each aspect of the assignment.

Not articulating marking criteria to parents and students can have negative consequences for the academic achievement of students and the professional autonomy of the teacher.

DETAILED MARKING RUBRIC

Aspect	F (0)	C- (1)	C (2)	B (3)	A (4)
Style (20%) Vocabulary Tone of voice	• often uses inappropriate tone • simple sentences • errors in word choice	• choppy writing • simple vocabulary • no sentence variety • undeveloped and informal	• no distinct tone or voice • occasionally uses informal language • some sophisticated vocabulary	• gaining distinct voice • uses formal language • variety of sentence types • appropriate vocabulary used	• unique style of writing • powerful vocabulary used • shows maturity and insight • takes risks with writing style
Form (40%) Analysis Organization and structure Transitions	• illogical or no structure • may omit several focus words • ideas not linked with transitions	• does not have all the focus words • few transitions • little analysis	• may be missing 1 or 2 focus words • weak transitions • some analysis	• well-organized • good use of transitions • logical • analyzes all focus words with clarity	• excellent use of transitions • creates strong flow • flawless logic and analysis • all parts addressed with insight/depth
Conventions (40%) Spelling Punctuation Grammar	• frequent noticeable errors that interfere with meaning	• many spelling, punctuation, and grammatical errors • clarity is obscured	• noticeable errors that are distracting • meaning is relatively clear	• some minor errors present, but do not interfere with meaning	• spelling, grammar, punctuation errors non-existent

In this rubric for an English course, note that values have been assigned to each aspect.

A teacher who marks outside the stated criteria runs the risk of appearing capricious and biased.

Evaluating Disruptive Behavior

Tim, a Grade 9 drama student, known for his high jinks and incessant chatter, was thrown out of the classroom by the teacher for wrestling with another student on the floor when he should have been practising a soliloquy. Despite this student's often-disruptive behavior, he performed his soliloquy almost flawlessly for the teacher the next day. Much to the dismay of Tim and his parents, Tim received a letter grade of C- for his performance, and a written comment by the teacher alluded to the fact that his low mark was the result of his disruptive and unruly behavior the previous day.

By following the stated marking criteria, a teacher enhances the public's perception that he or she is a fair and objective marker.

Clearly, this teacher would have difficulty justifying the mark awarded. If *attitude* were not mentioned as one of the marking criteria, then the student's disruptive behavior cannot be used for evaluation purposes. (Even if *attitude* were mentioned, the teacher might have difficulty demonstrating that this criterion is a valid measure of the course goals and content.) It would seem evident that the low mark was intended only to punish the student further. (For a discussion on writing valid criteria, see Chapter 2.)

Avoiding the Halo and the Pitchfork Effect

The *halo effect* is a teacher's tendency to increase a mark based only on a favorable impression of the student, rather than on the quality of the work. The *pitchfork effect* is seen when a teacher lowers a student's mark based on a negative impression of the student, perhaps caused by negative behaviors.

A detailed, analytical rubric allows the teacher to reduce the *halo effect* when marking. At times, teachers will raise a student's borderline mark, irrespective of the academic quality of the student's work, based on a general impression of the student. While most teachers try to mark all student work fairly and consistently, they at times are influenced by the personalities and appearances of their students. Simply put, some students are likeable and some are not. This phenomenon of teachers awarding higher marks to favorable students based on their personal feelings and impressions finds its counterpart in the *pitchfork effect*, which sees teachers lower a student's borderline mark should the student leave an unfavorable impression in the mind of the teacher due to negative behaviors, such as repeatedly disrupting class, displaying a poor attitude or work habit, or excessive tardiness. While marking tends to be faster using a holistic, global style of rubric like the sample on page 9, this rubric's lack of specificity tends to leave the teacher more susceptible to being influenced by irrelevant variables.

Marking criteria can be used by the teacher not only to inform a student and parent about what is expected in an answer, but also as a reference when a teacher wishes to justify his or her marks.

SAMPLE HOLISTIC MARKING RUBRIC

A   Superior (4)

- Meets all criteria developed in class
- Message or main idea is very clear
- Shows detailed planning and excellent organization
- Only one or two spelling, punctuation, and grammatical errors
- Makes insightful connections between concepts discussed in class and personal experiences

B   Good (3)

- Meets all criteria developed in class
- Message or main idea is presented
- Shows careful planning and organization
- Makes few errors in spelling, punctuation, and grammar
- Makes connections between concepts discussed in class and personal experiences

C   Satisfactory (2)

- Meets most of the criteria developed in class
- Attempts to present a message or main idea
- Shows an attempt at planning and organization
- Makes some errors in spelling, punctuation, and grammar
- Attempts to make a connection between concepts discussed in class and personal experiences

F   Fail (1)

- Meets few if any criteria developed in class
- Does not recognize or include a message or main idea
- Shows little, if any, planning and organization
- Makes numerous errors in spelling, punctuation, and grammar
- Does not make any connections between concepts discussed in class and personal experiences

Criteria used to evaluate a student's written essay in an English course.

TEACHER TIPS

- **Present students with the marking criteria when the work is first assigned.** The teacher must tell the students *how* the assignment will be marked. This requires the teacher to tell a student

  - what information or content is required, and
  - how the teacher will assign marks to this content.

In other words, parents and students must be informed if some content is worth more marks than other content.

- **Document the criteria in writing.** As with any written contract, the criteria can be used to settle disputes that might later arise. Also, students should receive their own copy of the criteria as a reference for completing their work.
- **Allow students to share in the development of the marking criteria.** Some teachers allow students to be part of the marking process and to contribute to the development of

Teachers may want to use the Marking Rubric (page 18) and Holistic Marking Rubric (page 19) templates to create and share marking criteria with students and parents. When students receive a copy of the marking criteria as the work is first assigned, they better understand the teacher's expectations and tend to assume greater responsibility for the successful completion of schoolwork.

criteria. This approach lets students see the relevance and importance of the criteria, and provides them with a sense of ownership, thereby possibly improving motivation. Also, some parents and administrators find it more difficult to question the mark assigned if they know that students had an active role in developing the criteria.

• **Do not change the marking criteria once they have been established.** If the teacher deviates from the marking criteria, perhaps to satisfy the demands of a single student, then he or she may be setting a precedent and have to repeat the behavior in the future.

• **Provide students with examples that fall within the various achievement categories.** Often, students and teachers do not share the same definitions regarding the quality of work. While the teacher might state that the student must "take risks with writing style" or use "powerful vocabulary" to receive an A, it may be unclear to the student what is meant by these behaviors. Indeed, different teachers may themselves interpret these criteria differently. By providing the class with examples that illustrate the various levels of achievement, students will have a better chance of meeting the teacher's expectation. This might mean, for example, that in an English class, the teacher would show and discuss previous student essays that represent each letter grade.

2. The Academic Level of Thought

The three components of evaluation:
1. a stated *criteria level*
2. the *academic level of thought*
3. a *statement of conditions*

The second component of the marking process is the *academic level of thought*. Before assigning any task, the teacher must determine the level of thought expected from a student. Does the teacher expect the answer to be simply descriptive and factual, or must the student's answer go into more depth and perhaps be critical and analytical? If evaluation is to reflect the student's level of learning, then it stands to reason that a teacher should not evaluate the student beyond classroom instruction.

A teacher's assignments can be classified as belonging to different levels of academic complexity and sophistication. The level of thought that is to be exhibited by the student is also referred to as the *cognitive domain*.

The Cognitive Level of Instruction

Mr. K, an elementary-school history teacher, had a complaint filed against him by the parents of one of his students. The complainants noted to the superintendent of schools that Mr. K assigned daily activities that required students only to memorize and recall facts, but that he evaluated student learning using activities that required critical analysis and logical reasoning. The superintendent concluded that Mr. K's classroom instruction and activities did not cognitively prepare students for the more sophisticated demands required for the successful completion of later tasks and assignments.

When marking an assignment, the teacher needs to recognize the verbs used in the assignment task. For example, these two sample essay questions (or tasks) require two very different types of responses from students:

Question #1: *Identify* the methods of hunting and gathering used in the Jomon Period of Ancient Japan.

Question #2: *Justify* and *defend* the hunting and gathering methods used in the Jomon Period of Ancient Japan.

In the first question, the teacher expects a student's answer simply to list facts and to be descriptive. This is evident from the use of the action word *identify*. However, in the second question, the teacher expects a student's answer to be more sophisticated and to go beyond a simple description. The words *justify* and *defend* indicate that the teacher expects the answer to express a personal judgment, and that the student will defend these judgments. In short, the two questions require very different types of answers, thus requiring the teacher to evaluate the work accordingly.

In all academic subjects, there are six different levels of academic thought, or complexity, used to classify a student's academic work. A student's work may be classified under the following six cognitive categories:

1. the *knowledge* level
2. the *comprehension* level
3. the *application* level
4. the *analysis* level
5. the *synthesis* level
6. the *evaluation* level

The Knowledge Level

The simplest type of answer a student can create belongs to the knowledge level. This type of answer requires the student to remember or recall information, such as facts, rules, or problem-solving strategies. Some action words commonly used at the knowledge level are

arrange	recall	name	repeat
quote	describe	relate	reproduce
order	match	label	tabulate
define	recognize	outline	recite
list	identify	state	select

By looking at the action verb used by the teacher in the assignment or question, the student will recognize that the teacher expects the answer to be at the knowledge level. For example, in this essay question, the action word *identify* informs the student that his answer should be limited to the recall and listing of facts:

Identify the hunting and gathering methods used in the Jomon Period of Ancient Japan.

The Comprehension Level

The next level—comprehension—requires the student to change the form of communication: to interpret facts, re-state what he or she sees, translate knowledge into a new context, reach conclusions, and see consequences. Some action verbs used by teachers for this level are

alter	explain	give	report
defend	contrast	generalize	paraphrase
estimate	discriminate	discuss	predict
classify	extend	infer	
distinguish	convert	summarize	

At this level, a teacher's assignment question might resemble this one:

Explain why there are different methods of hunting and gathering in the Jomon Period of Ancient Japan.

In this case, the teacher would expect the student's answer to be more than just a simple collection of facts. Rather, the student would be required to make inferences, or conclusions, from the course material. At this level of thought, it would be a mistake for a teacher to evaluate the question at the knowledge level.

The Application Level

Questions written at the *application level* require the student to use previously acquired information in a new setting and in a way that is different from the original context. This means the student should not try to rely on the original context in which the problem was learned. Some action verbs found at this level are

apply	choose	develop	show
demonstrate	make	model	utilize
prepare	relate	transfer	produce
compute	classify	draw	interpret
experiment	manage	organize	
discover	solve	use	

The above sample question may be modified to fit the application level:

Demonstrate how the hunting and gathering methods of the Jomon people could be applied to solve modern-day subsistence needs.

Here, the student is required to go beyond the original context in which the material was first learned and to solve the problem using the skills and knowledge learned in class.

The Analysis Level

The analysis level requires the student to identify logical errors, to point out contradictions, or to differentiate among facts, opinions, hypotheses, assumptions, and conclusions. The student is expected to draw relationships among ideas. Some action verbs are

analyze	outline	differentiate	point out
break down	associate	illustrate	separate out
separate	diagram	conclude	conclude
ascertain	distinguish	relate	
deduce	compare	infer	

An example question would be

Point out the shortcomings of the hunting and gathering methods of the Jomon people, given the changing climatic conditions of Ancient Japan.

The Synthesis Level

The synthesis level requires the student to create something unique or original, and may require the student's answer or product to use a combination of ideas to form a new whole. Some action words are

categorize	compose	construct	synthesize
design	integrate	invent	hypothesize
predict	pose	integrate	organize
compile	combine	create	
devise	expand	formulate	
produce	plan	theorize	

At the synthesis level, the teacher may ask the students to do something like this:

Design an experiment that shows that the hunting and gathering methods of the Jomon people were sufficient to support the subsistence needs of a tribe.

At this level, the student is expected to combine parts to arrive at a unique product, to connect knowledge from several different areas, to use old ideas to create new ones, and to make conclusions from given facts.

The Evaluation Level

Finally, the most complex level—evaluation—requires the student to form judgments and make decisions about the value of ideas, methods, people, or products, and to be able to state the reasons for these judgments. Some action verbs are

assess	defend	support	judge
criticize	deduce	contrast	recommend
justify	compare	evaluate	verify
appraise	decide	validate	

A sample task might be

Given the changing climate of Ancient Japan, *judge* the effectiveness of the Jomon hunting and gathering methods.

The above task would require the student explicitly to state the criteria or reasons that were used to reach a particular conclusion. The student would have to compare and discriminate between ideas, assess the value of ideas and theories, recognize bias, and verify evidence.

THE LEVELS OF THOUGHT

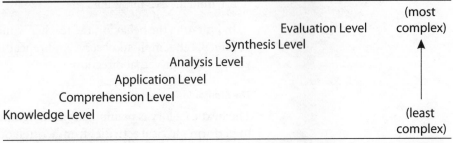

Before marking any assignment, the teacher must identify which one of the six cognitive levels of thought is being evaluated.

The Psychomotor Level of Performance

A Physical Activity to Measure a Cognitive Ability

A teacher of English literature intended to evaluate her students' abilities to read and understand a descriptive passage from an Old English text of Chaucer's *The Canterbury Tales*. The teacher asked the students to read one of the tales and then to draw an accurate picture of one of the story's characters from Chaucer's descriptive writing. One student, though she could read well and understand Chaucer's writing, could not draw well. Consequently, she received a low mark for the assignment. The teacher, when she was approached by the student, stated that the evaluation method was fair and accurate.

The problem here is that the teacher tried to measure the student's academic, cognitive comprehension using a physical activity. Essentially, this is similar to someone trying to use kilograms to measure the distance between two objects. Teachers of academic courses should evaluate students using activities that fall within the cognitive domains. For those courses, such as physical education and art, that do require the evaluation of physical and muscular skills, the teacher should rely on tasks that fall within the psychomotor domain. This domain has five levels of performance:

1. the *imitation* level
2. the *manipulation* level
3. the *precision* level
4. the *articulation* level
5. the *naturalization* level

The Imitation Level

The simplest psychomotor level is imitation. At this level, the student is expected to imitate, perhaps imperfectly, an action that is observed. Some action words are

align	grasp
hold	rest on
balance	copy
follow	repeat

At this stage, the teacher can expect the students' actions to be crude or clumsy, and to lack precision. For example, a physical education teacher might present students with the following task:

Copy the wrist and finger positions modeled by the teacher when shooting a basketball from the free-throw line.

In imitating the behavior, the teacher would not expect the students to display accuracy, but simply to observe and repeat the action demonstrated based on a visual model or verbal directions.

The Manipulation Level

The next category is manipulation. Assignments at this level require the student to perform physical activities from written or verbal instructions without the use of a model to copy. The student's performance may lack grace and coordination. Verbs at this level are the same as those at the imitation level, except that the student may follow spoken or written directions. At this level, the task might look like this:

Using the picture shown in the textbook, *imitate* the wrist and finger positions shown when shooting a basketball from the free-throw line.

The Precision Level

The level of precision requires the student to perform a physical activity without a model or directions. Students are expected to reproduce the action with few, if any, errors. Descriptive words associated with this level include

accurately	proficiently
with control	without error

An example from a physical education class might be

Accurately holding the basketball in the dominant hand with the wrist and fingers in the correct positions, shoot the basketball into the hoop from the free-throw line.

In this task, the teacher would expect the student's action to occur with control and a degree of refinement.

The Articulation Level

The level of articulation requires the student to perform a series of related acts in the proper order and sequence with accuracy, speed, and timing. Sample words include

coordination	timing
speed	integration
confidence	stability

At this level, a task might require students to

Shoot the basketball into the hoop using proper *coordination* of the upper body, eight times out of ten, within a two-minute time period.

The Naturalization Level

Assignments and tasks at the naturalization level require the student to perform as if the behavior is routine, automatic, and natural, with the appearance that little energy is being exerted. Action words include

naturally	professionally
effortlessly	routinely
spontaneously	automatically

An example task might be

During a basketball game, *spontaneously* and *effortlessly* shoot the basketball into the hoop with 80% accuracy when between the baseline and the three-point shooting line.

At this level, the student is expected to be able to repeat the behavior regularly and spontaneously.

3. A Statement of Conditions

A Case of Racism?

Ms. D, a Grade 7 teacher, gave her students the following essay assignment: *Using the articles distributed in class, state whether Aboriginal peoples should be given special rights to fishing.* Breanna, a bright and enthusiastic student, submitted an essay response she believed went above and beyond the requirements of the assignment. In writing the assignment, Breanna had visited and interviewed numerous representatives from Aboriginal groups, researched primary historical documents, pasted photos and documents in her essay, and had written almost twice as many pages as any of the other students. Breanna was shocked to the point of tears when, a week later, the teacher returned her essay with a grade of C. In a complaint to the principal, Breanna accused the teacher of blatant marking bias and outright racism. Breanna also expressed her firm belief that her lower-than-expected grade was due to the fact that Ms. D hated people who disagreed with her.

The three components of evaluation:
1. a stated *criteria level*
2. the *academic level of thought*
3. a *statement of conditions*

The point of any evaluation is to measure student learning *in relation to curricular content*; consequently, the teacher must often narrow the students' focus to direct students to the teacher's desired outcomes. The third component of the marking process requires the teacher to state clearly the conditions under which learning can be expected to occur. In other words, the teacher must state the use of specific tools, resources, materials, or locations needed to complete the assignment. In the case of Breanna, the teacher was able to dismiss the student's accusations as groundless by referring to the stipulated conditions of learning. A statement of conditions is important as it helps to focus the topic to be studied and prevents students from studying irrelevant material. This example task lacks a required statement of conditions:

Identify the conditions in the South that led to the Civil War in the United States.

No focus or context exists for the students—some students might identify geographical factors, some might look at social and racial concerns, and some might choose to identify economic issues. However, when the teacher adds a statement of conditions, the student's focus and point of view will likely match the teacher's expectations:

Using the map of strategic resources handed out in class, identify the conditions in the South that led to the Civil War in the United States.

As seen in the case of Breanna, for younger students it usually is prudent for the teacher to state explicitly the conditions of learning in the assignment task.

The phrase "Using the map of strategic resources handed out in class" is the necessary condition expected by the teacher for a student to get an A on the assignment. Also, since course assignments often are designed to prepare students for examinations, a statement of conditions informs the student what material will likely be covered on upcoming tests. Sometimes, the expected conditions are obvious and do not need to be stated directly. If conditions are stated in the course outline or in the course goals, they may not need to be stated again in the assignment question or task.

The Teacher's Feedback and Comments

A teacher's feedback and comments on all assignments should be immediate, specific, and prescriptive.

Most people, if they saw a child repeatedly banging his head against a brick wall, would try to stop the harmful behavior. If the child told us he did it because it feels good when he stops, we would take him to have his head examined. If an educator allows students to make the same errors on their assignments time and time again without providing corrective measures, only because the students do not complain and seem satisfied with their marks, then that educator's professional judgment may be called into question.

If a student is to improve his or here academic standing, then the teacher must provide guidance and explain to the student why full marks were not given. The teacher's feedback and comments on all assignments should be immediate, specific, and prescriptive. Even if the student has performed well, it is not sufficient for the teacher simply to write "*Good*" as a comment; rather, the student must know what was good about the work. Students who do not receive teacher feedback relatively soon after submitting their work are likely to repeat the detrimental behavior, and to experience academic and motivational setbacks. The longer the delay in feedback, the less likely the student will learn from the activity. Indeed, it is often difficult for a teacher to justify teaching and evaluating a new concept when students have not been informed of previous learning mistakes.

Corrective Feedback

An elementary-school science teacher, after three weeks of instruction on the scientific method, gave a culminating activity that required students to create and conduct a laboratory experiment using the principles discussed in class. The final student product was to be written up in a formal report and submitted to the teacher for 20 marks. One student named Mike designed an experiment that measured the influence of sunlight on plant growth. Mike submitted his work and the teacher took several weeks to mark it. However, in the interim, Mike's parents requested that the teacher provide their son and his classmates with supplemental material to reinforce the concept of the scientific method. The teacher complied with this request, but was taken aback when Mike's parents demanded that this supplemental work be included in the teacher's record of marks. The teacher refused the request and explained his reasoning: since students had not yet been informed of their mistakes and weaknesses on the culminating assignment, they might repeat these same mistakes on subsequent work that measured the same outcomes. Thus, students could possibly be penalized twice for the same unspecified, uncorrected errors.

Marking Rubric

Assignment Title: _____

	F ( )	C- ( )	C ( )	B ( )	A ( )
Criterion 1					
Criterion 2					
Criterion 3					
Criterion 4					

Holistic Marking Rubric

Assignment Title: _____

( ) Exceeds Expectations

-
-
-
-

( ) Fully Meets Expectations

-
-
-
-

( ) Minimally Meets Expectations

-
-
-
-

( ) Does Not Yet Meet Expectations

-
-
-
-

( ) Fails

-
-
-

Course Goals and Objectives

Roller Coasters and Amusement Parks

A Grade 7 teacher found herself increasingly confronted by angry parents demanding to know why she and her students were not covering the same topics and content as students in the same grade level in the class across the hall. These parents wanted to know, for example, why she was teaching about roller coasters and taking her students on field trips to the amusement park while the more senior, experienced Grade 7 teacher was giving lessons on astronomy and having students solve calculation problems on worksheets. The parents worried that the students of this less-experienced teacher were not learning important concepts, and that this would negatively affect their performance on the upcoming final examination.

How to Decide What to Teach

The curriculum guide details the skills, attitudes, and abilities society deems important for students to possess.

Occasionally, administrators and teachers witness parents, some bordering on hysteria, express concern that their children are not going to be adequately prepared to meet the challenges of the next academic year because they are not studying the same topics as their counterparts in another classroom. The reason teachers at the same grade level teach different topics is simply because they can. For each course at each grade level, teachers are required to follow a basic blueprint of what to teach. This blueprint—essentially a brief, somewhat vague outline of the course content—is the curriculum guide, and it details the skills, attitudes, and abilities that society deems important for students to possess if they are to be active, contributing members of society.

The Sample Curriculum Page on page 21 shows a sample from a curriculum guide for a high-school English course. As can be seen, the curriculum guide is made up of individual, rather non-specific points that must be taught. These are called *goals*. Goals are deliberately vague in order to make them more amenable to the needs of local student interests and abilities, school resources, and teacher experience and expertise. Teachers also have a great deal of flexibility in choosing the methods they will use to teach these goals, the specific content of the academic topics, and the complexity of the learning activities. For example, in a physics class, a teacher may address the goal "students will create and interpret line graphs" by teaching lessons that deal with sports, while another physics teacher may choose to teach this same goal by talking about space travel.

Teachers do not have the luxury of picking and choosing which goals will be taught. Those teachers who do not teach all of the required goals of a course—and are caught—usually lay blame on time constraints and the burden of having too many professional duties. Truth be told, this failure is more likely the result of poor planning on the part of the teacher, and could prove to be a chink in the teacher's professional armor should parents or administrators become aware of it. A teacher who does not teach all of the prescribed goals is doing a disservice to the students, especially if those students later must write district-wide standardized tests.

SAMPLE CURRICULUM PAGE

By the end of the year, it is expected that students will be able to

1. demonstrate an understanding of the main ideas and plots of stories
2. explain the motivation and point of view of different characters in stories
3. share details with other students regarding the stories and articles read
4. revise and edit their writings
5. write a variety of fiction and non-fiction compositions using logical thought
6. apply the conventions of the English language, using proper grammar, spelling, and punctuation

A page from a sample English curriculum guide showing course goals.

Strategies for Using Course Goals and Curriculum Guides

1. Make sure that academic marks and assignments reflect the goals in the curriculum guide. A student's marks must reflect his or her understanding of the curriculum guide's goals. Therefore, a teacher would not be able to assign marks based on things such as attitude and attendance if these were not goals found in the curriculum guide. A teacher could base part of a course's final grade on student attendance only if the curriculum guide for that course stated that attendance is to be taught in that course; however, a teacher would have a difficult time convincing parents and administrators that attendance in some way can be used to measure a student's comprehension of a course goal.

In this case, it is clear that assigning a mark to a student simply for completing an exercise, irrespective of proficiency, undermines the purpose of marks and letter grades.

Assigning Marks for Homework Completion

A chemistry student received a year-end score of 87.4%; he needed a score of 90% to get an A. The teacher checked student homework during every class and gave marks to students for homework completion, which accounted for 10% of the final course mark. This student frequently did not complete his homework and, therefore, was given a low mark for his homework completion. The student's parents filed a complaint with the principal and argued that the teacher made an error in evaluation when he gave marks to students simply for completing their homework. They said that the teacher should have based the homework marks on the quality of the students' answers, and that homework completion in no way reflected their son's comprehension of the curriculum guide's goals and the course content. They argued further that homework completion is related to a student's motivation and time-management skills, and not to the chemistry course goals. The principal concluded that the parents were correct and that the teacher should not have awarded marks based on whether or not the student did his homework, but on whether or not the student did the homework correctly. Subsequently, the teacher was required to remove the category *homework completion* from his marks book and the student received an A for the course.

2. Be familiar with school policies regarding the deduction of marks for late student work. Whether to deduct marks for late assignments is somewhat of a gray area for most teachers and administrators. Logically, given the above assertion that a grade must reflect the goals of the curriculum guide, the argument could be made that a student should not lose marks for late work. However, practicality would seem to dictate otherwise. Not deducting "late marks" could present teachers with an unmanageable marking situation, since many students, feeling little pressure to respect due dates, would turn in a glut of unmarked work at the end of the school year.

> Since the curriculum guide is a public document, readily obtained by anyone, teachers could find themselves in a compromising position should they encounter a keen parent who is more familiar with the document than the teacher.

3. Thoroughly read and be familiar with the curriculum guide and the goals for the course or subject. The curriculum guide is a public document and a copy can be obtained from the principal or the school board. Teachers should preview the guide early in the academic year to justify the content and skills that will be taught and the marks awarded—course planning will be enhanced and the teacher will appear more knowledgeable and confident when talking to administrators and parents.

4. Make sure there is a logical connection between any assignment and a related course goal. If a teacher cannot see how a particular assignment helps to achieve a course goal in the curriculum guide, or a goal in the course outline, then the activity can not rationally be used for grading purposes.

An Irrelevant Evaluation Activity

A teacher of foods and nutrition wanted to assess the students' understanding of the following goal: *students will understand the connection between diet and physical health.* She had the students record their daily meals in a journal. At the end of a four-week period, she timed the students as they ran around the school. She awarded marks based on the students' speed compared to their recorded times earlier in the year. After several complaints from parents and students, the teacher admitted that there was no connection between the learning activity (running) and the stated goal. The teacher also admitted that she incorrectly used a psychomotor domain to measure an academic goal. Students were re-assessed using a different, more appropriate assignment.

---

5. Find out if the school district has and uses *performance standards.* Marking criteria can also be influenced by standards established by school districts. Performance standards inform the teacher how well students are expected to perform on assignments and tests. Performance standards may accompany curriculum guides or they may exist as a separate document. They may also state, in general terms, what the student's performance should look like for each letter grade in the different subjects. In theory, this means that all the teachers using the same set of performance standards to grade students would all agree as to what a student would need to exhibit in order to receive an A. Thus, the implication is that all students throughout the school district who receive an A based on the same performance standards in the same course would all possess similar skills and knowledge.

> *Performance standards* are established by school districts to standardize, or make uniform, the meaning of each letter grade.

6. Create a year plan. As the label implies, a year plan is a brief overview of the monthly concepts and goals to be taught. A year plan provides course direction and allows the teacher to demonstrate that all the required course goals have been addressed.

When planning the school year, the teacher may use the Monthly Year Plan on page 32, which requires that a separate page be used for each month and for each course. This year plan has the advantage of allowing the teacher to detail the goals, objectives, and concepts to be taught. The Full Year Plan on pages 33–34 provides a brief overview of the entire year at a glance, but it allows the teacher to list only narrowly the concepts to be taught for each month. It has the advantage of allowing numerous subjects or courses to be addressed in one document.

The Course Goals Checklist on page 35 allows the teacher to ensure that all the goals of the curriculum guide have been addressed, while also informing students and parents of the goals that a particular letter grade represents. Course goals and their related unit, or the date on which they were addressed, may be listed in advance of instruction, or may be recorded as they are completed.

In order to make curriculum-guide goals teachable, they must be broken down into several specific goals, called *objectives*.

7. Make sure that it is clear which individual goals are represented by a report-card mark. The teacher must know which goals have been taught and which goals the student's letter grade reflects. A letter grade does not simply reflect the scores obtained on individual assignments; rather, it represents a student's ability to reach the specific goals that have been taught. This is the reason why a student who is caught plagiarizing on an assignment or cheating on a test can not be given a failing grade for the entire course, if the assignment or test measures only a narrow spectrum of goals.

Cheating on a Test

Duncan, a student of average ability, was under a great deal of pressure from his parents to achieve high academic marks. The teacher caught Duncan cheating on his math test—Duncan had crib notes written on a little scrap of paper he kept in the palm of his hand. When Duncan's parents were informed of their son's transgression, they agreed with the teacher that their son had made a serious error in judgment, but the teacher was stunned by the parents' subsequent demand. Duncan's parents believed that to spare the rod was to spoil the child—metaphorically speaking—and that, if Duncan were truly to appreciate the consequences of his action, then he must receive a failing grade on his next report card. Despite the teacher's objections to this demand, Duncan's parents were insistent and approached the principal regarding the matter.

In the case of poor Duncan, both the teacher and the principal recognized that the parents, though having the best of intentions for their child, were ill-informed. The principal agreed with the teacher that it was appropriate for the student to receive a failing grade on only the one test on which he had cheated. The principal further noted, "Letter grades can not be used to punish students, and may be used only to reflect a student's learning and comprehension of the program goals and objectives."

Objectives

I have heard it said, "Love is never having to say 'I love you'." Well, perhaps this is true. Either we know someone loves us, or we do not, and no single test or statement can validate love's existence. Even the most straightforward declaration of love often has little meaning. Curriculum guide goals are a little like saying "I love you." In and of themselves, they are actually quite hollow and meaningless. Indeed, how would a student know if he truly understands "the main ideas and plots of stories" or that she sufficiently understands "the motivation and point of view of different characters," as stated in goals number 1 and 2 in the sample curriculum on page 21? In order to rectify the potential for ambiguity and to make the curriculum guide goals "teachable," the educator must turn a general goal into several specific goals, or objectives. For example, the teacher might take the general curriculum goal "students will know the meaning of vocabulary words" and break it down into three narrower, more manageable specific goals:

Students will be able to write the definitions for the words with 90% accuracy.
Students will be able to identify correct antonyms for 80% of the words.
Students will be able to write sentences that use the words correctly 90% of the time.

These more specific objectives now may be taught over a series of lessons. Also, in order for the teacher to know when and if the students understand the concept, the teacher must quantify the behavior, determining how much of the behavior must be demonstrated by students in order to say that they have successfully reached the curriculum guide goal. For example, how would a physical education teacher giving a lesson on the proper technique of hitting a baseball know if he had successfully taught the skill to his students? To address this concern, the teacher may state in his specific objective that the skill is attained only when a student is able to hit nine out of ten pitches (90%).

It is not sufficient that a teacher simply knows what broad curriculum-guide goal is being addressed in a lesson. Rather, teachers must know what specific behavior they are asking their students to perform. If the goal requires the student to "know the meaning of vocabulary words," then the teacher—and the students, too—must be clear what "to know" looks like. In other words, the student behavior must be *operationalized*. It is unacceptable for a teacher to say, for example, that students will be marked on their "understanding" of the topic, or on the "quality" of their work. What does "understanding" mean? What does "quality" look like? How will the teacher recognize these student behaviors? A teacher cannot observe and assess "understanding," but can observe and assess a specific, quantifiable student behavior, which then can be reported to the student's parents. This also means that school report-card grades must reflect assignments and test marks, and not be based on abstract notions of thought processes.

A goal is operationalized when the student behavior is stated in specific terms that can be observed and measured.

A Grade Based on Intuition

A teacher-in-training from a local college was assigned the responsibility of issuing report-card marks to the students of an English class she had been teaching for three months. One student earned 90% (an A) in the course during the reporting period. The teacher-in-training, however, suggested that the student not "count his chickens before they hatched"; in her opinion, he did not truly and fully understand the course content at an A level and, therefore, was not truly an A student. The classroom teacher-advisor, who oversaw the daily performance of the student-teacher, clarified that a report-card grade must reflect the student's scores achieved on individual evaluation items. The teacher-advisor further explained that if marks do not reflect the student's level of achievement, then the original marking criteria may need to be adjusted. He went on to advise the teacher-in-training that parents and students should feel confident that assignment marks reflect a student's level of understanding, and that they should not be faced with the surprise of a report-card mark that is greatly lower than expected.

A student's "way of thinking" can be evaluated only when it is operationalized and expressed in the form of a product. The teacher can defend the grading of a student only when evaluations are based on the tangible, concrete work of the student. For this reason, activities that fall within the affective domain—which takes into account a student's interests, values, and attitudes—should be approached with caution when quantifying a student's performance. While the affective component is crucial to a student's mental and social development, it consists of "fuzzy" concepts—creativity, appreciation, and respect—that are difficult to define and which tend to result in low inter-rater reliability. Indeed, the affective domain should be expressed and measured only through a product or specific task.

Measuring the Affective Domain

A Grade 7 teacher asked her students to write a poem that expresses "the beauty and joy of nature," and to write the poem in a way that would allow the reader to share their feelings. One father complained about the mark his son received and the teacher comment, "Your poem just describes killing a bug. Boring!" on the back of his son's work. The teacher tried to defend the mark she awarded by noting that the child's poem did not display an ability to satisfactorily fulfill the unit goal of "appreciating that poetry can be used to express personal emotions." The father disagreed; so did the principal. Essentially, the principal's reasoning followed the poetic belief that beauty is in the eye of the beholder.

Creating Criteria

The criteria being marked must be aligned with and lead to the objective and goal being measured.

Academic goals are achieved only through the presentation of thoughtfully developed classroom activities, and it is the teacher's marking criteria that serve as the linchpin between the two. When deciding appropriate marking criteria, it is essential that the teacher select only those features that are central to the skill being evaluated, and does not simply select those features that are the most easily observed. The criteria being marked must be aligned with and lead to the objective and goal being measured. As seen in Sample Marking Criteria on page 26, the criteria reflect those aspects of the activity that deal with, for example, the desired behavior of *analysis*. Also, trivial and unrelated aspects of performance should not be evaluated, as seen in the case Evaluating Irrelevant Criteria.

Evaluating Irrelevant Criteria

A biology student complained to his teacher that the mark he received on his poster assignment was too low. The teacher, in her first year of teaching, told the student that, according to the marking criteria discussed in class, it was a fair mark. Also, the teacher reminded the student that the class was informed of the marking criteria when the work was first assigned. Dissatisfied, the student discussed the matter with his school counsellor. The counsellor noted that some of the marking criteria used for the assignment were irrelevant and in no way contributed to an accurate evaluation of the student's understanding of the course topics. (For example, one of the teacher's criteria was that students must use a red-colored poster board.) Upon being informed of the counsellor's concerns, the biology teacher agreed that several of her stated marking criteria were in no way relevant to the goals or topic being evaluated. The teacher also agreed that publicly stating a marking criterion to the students does not necessarily make it a legitimate criterion.

A basic rule of thumb is that good criteria reflect those skills that experts consider the most important aspects of the concept. This means that one way a teacher can justify the choice of marking criteria is to relate them to pre-existing rubrics or standards written by school district personnel, publishers, or other teachers. However, teachers also must be careful not to cling too dogmatically to

Unit Title: Industrial Revolution

Unit Goal: Analyze bias in pictures

Activity Task: Using the cartoon labelled "Hard at Work" analyze and discuss two ethical issues the artist raises regarding the social classes in 18th-century England.

Marking Criteria	Marks
• Identifies 2 ethical concerns expressed by the artist	9–10
• Differentiates the artist's point of view from the observations of other commentators	
• Points out the artist's biases using specific evidence from the cartoon	
• Relates these issues to the exploitation of the working class	
• Identifies 2 ethical issues expressed by the artist	7–8
• Outlines the artist's beliefs regarding social reform	
• Points out specific evidence in the cartoon that displays the artist's bias	
• Identifies 2 ethical issues expressed by the artist	5–6
• States why these might be concerns of the artist	
• Relates the issues to the working class	
• Identifies 2 ethical concerns expressed by the artist	3–4
• States why these issues might be concerns of the artist	
• Identifies 2 ethical concerns with no relevant discussion	1–2

Aspects of *analyze* are reflected in the descriptions

The marking criteria link the activity to the desired goal or objective.

their criteria and fail to recognize the occasional creative student response that may not fit existing marking categories, but that, nonetheless, displays a keen understanding of the concepts and skills.

The Value of Unit Plans

Students—even very young students—tend quite naturally to pick up and bandy about terms and phrases that they hear in adult conversation, even if they do not fully understand the meaning. The term *unit* is one such word that has made the jump from the professional talk of teachers to student-initiated conversations. Most students, and even some parents, are aware that a unit is a group of lessons that deal with a single topic of study and that usually lasts from two to six weeks. Units are a way to organize lessons around a common theme, such as Ancient Rome, China, government, or even pizza making. However, a unit is more than simply a topic of study; it is a way for the teacher to organize lessons that represent related goals found in the curriculum guide. The reverse is also true, as units allow the teacher to organize all the course goals into discrete instructional packages, thereby helping to ensure that all the required goals will be covered during the course of the academic year.

Unit plans may be created by school district employees or the classroom teacher, or be bought at educational supply stores.

SAMPLE UNIT PLAN ON ANCIENT EGYPT

Title: Ancient Egypt

Course: History

Time: 4 to 5 weeks

Objectives:

By the end of the unit, students will be able to

1. define and identify three classes of Ancient Egyptian society;

2. illustrate ways in which man has changed and is capable of changing his environment by comparing Ancient Egyptian practices with modern-day agricultural practices;

3. recognize that social harmony led to agricultural mass production and the development of the state;

4. recognize that societies often rely on other societies for prosperity, by analyzing Ancient Egyptian trade practices and routes;

5. understand the differences between primary and secondary resources by writing a research report.

Content Outline:

1. The Land of Egypt
    - location
    - environment
    - origins of the people
2. The Nile River
    - physical characteristics
    - flooding and farming
3. The Old Kingdom
    - Menes and unification
    - religion
    - pyramids
    - the class system
4. Middle Kingdom
    - nomads and conflict
    - the Hyksos
5. The New Kingdom
    - Hatshepsut
    - Thutmose III
    - monotheism
    - Tutankhamen

Activities:

- class discussion
- students create a Nile board game
- students make a model of Blue and White Nile
- class debate
- students create a time capsule

Evaluation:

- worksheets
- student-made clay project
- descriptive essay
- unit test

This is more than just an outline of the content to be taught, since it uses objectives to organize and deliver related course goals. Only later in the unit, during individual lessons, will the teacher publicly state the specific marking criteria for any assignment.

The Numerical Value Assigned to Goals and Units

Most people have likely had a dream in which they are trying to run down a path, but are unable to coordinate their legs to simulate motion; the faster one tries to run, the more rooted to the same spot one feels. To be sure, such dreams can be frustrating. A teacher who evaluates the same goal in three or four different academic units may be subjecting students to a similar perpetual, real-life, evaluation nightmare, as that one goal may be over-represented in the marking process, thus unfairly under-representing the students' true abilities. For example, a student in a physical education course who has trouble meeting the goal "students will be able to perform a somersault" would be unfairly penalized if this one goal kept popping up during every instructional unit.

Teachers must be careful not to assign a significantly higher numerical value to one unit over other units unless there is a clear, logical reason for doing so. The teacher must be able to provide a logical rationale for the numerical values that are assigned to the various goals and objectives.

The Value Assigned to Units

During a routine formal evaluation of a teacher's classroom performance, the school administrator questioned the teacher regarding the values she assigned to the various units she taught in the course. The administrator noted that one unit on *Chance and Probability* was assigned a value of 80 marks, while another unit on *Logarithmic Scales* was given a value of only 30 marks. It was further noted that both units covered the same number of goals. The principal requested the teacher to provide a rationale as to why one unit had almost three times the value of the other.

The teacher knew that numerical scores cannot arbitrarily and randomly be assigned to various categories, and that the value assigned to any category must be supported by sound educational reasoning. Any teacher who is in a similar situation should consider the following factors when deciding the numerical value of units or course objectives:

1. The skills and concepts that receive the most instructional time in the classroom receive the highest weight.
2. Activities that require the student to use higher-level thinking (analysis, synthesis, evaluation) usually receive a greater weight than activities that rely on lower-level thinking (knowledge, comprehension, application).
3. Activities that assess more important and numerous goals tend to receive heavier weights.
4. Activities that are less objective and open to different interpretations receive a lower weight.

The Lesson Plan

A Teacher without Lesson Plans

The students enrolled in an English class and their parents became concerned when the teacher began each lesson with the question, "So, what shall we do today?" This teacher, though well-liked and respected by other teachers in the school, never kept a daybook that outlined the day's activities and sequence of instruction. During an investigation by the principal, the teacher defended himself by noting that his years of teaching experience did not require him to write lesson plans. However, a disciplinary review panel concluded that the teacher's failure to write and compile lesson plans was not in accordance with professional conduct for the following reasons: "1) a substitute teacher entering the classroom would likely be unable to teach the lesson since no instructional plans exist; 2) the absence of lesson plans suggests the existence of poor organizational skills and teaching inefficiency; and 3) evidence does not exist that course goals are being taught."

A teacher who enters the classroom without a lesson plan to guide the delivery of the course goals is putting his or her position at risk with the principal, parents, and students.

With its roots in child psychology studies and its refinement through decades of classroom practice, the lesson plan is more than just a step-by-step list of instructions for the efficient teaching of concepts. Collectively, a teacher's daily lesson plans constitute a log book, which can be referred to by the teacher at a later date should specific classroom events be called into question. The daybook's entries provide written evidence that the course goals have been taught and that they have been taught in a pedagogically sound manner.

While lesson and unit plans are not public documents and do not need to be shared with parents and students, principals often do have the right to review and preview a teacher's instructional plans. (In fact, it is not uncommon for many principals occasionally and surreptitiously to enter a teacher's classroom after hours to read the next day's lessons.) In Photographs and "Lost" Assignments (below), the teacher's assiduous record keeping of daily instructional events allowed her to defend her marking decisions when confronted by concerned parents and an administrator.

Photographs and "Lost" Assignments

A Grade 12 geography student and his parents filed a complaint with the school principal in which they stated that the student's report-card mark of C- was the direct result of the teacher constantly losing the student's work over a three-month period. As proof that the student had completed the teacher's assigned work, the parents proffered the claim that they had secretly been photographing each and every piece of the student's work prior to it being submitted for a mark. The parents went on to claim that the teacher's lessons were unstructured and ineffective, and that the student's work was not being marked in a timely manner. In an interview with the principal, the teacher was able to refer to her lesson plans to show 1) the exact day the class work was collected and returned to the students; 2) that this particular student had been given an opportunity to rewrite the assignments, but chose not to; 3) that this particular student's work was incomplete when initially turned in; and 4) that the course goals and concepts were being taught in an educationally sound manner. Not surprisingly, photographs of missing geography work never made an appearance.

Lesson plans are not only a recipe for the teacher's successful delivery of instruction, but they help teachers to ensure that the end-of-lesson activity appropriately evaluates student learning. In the following case, an uninformed parent questions the evaluative worth of a teacher's classroom activities.

See the Sample Lesson Plan on Ancient Egypt on page 30 for the structure of a typical lesson plan.

The Evaluation Activity

Mrs. O, a member of the school Parent Action Committee, believed that her son's report-card grade of C was the direct result of the teacher's evaluation activities. In Mrs. O's estimation, the teacher's activities were nonsensical and frivolous, and did not reflect her son's "true God-given talents." In a letter to the principal, Mrs. O expressed her belief that the teacher's classroom activities trivialized learning and that "singing songs and creating ridiculous [*sic*] skits" did not reflect the high academic standards that the parents of the community had come to expect from teachers at the school. Mrs. O demanded that the teacher rely less on game playing and more on "traditional paper-and-pencil exercises."

In order to motivate students and to make learning fun, teachers will often employ learning activities that, to the untrained eye, may appear to be off the mark. In the case of Mrs. O, the teacher had only to refer to his lesson plan to show that the stated evaluation activity did indeed reflect and lead to his stated objective.

One must remember that the teacher's task is to address the curriculum guide goals and, to achieve this, the teacher must create an operationalized objective that is specific to the lesson. In order for the teacher to know if students have attained this objective, he or she must clearly state the required criteria in the objective, and do so once again in the evaluation section located at the end of the written lesson plan. As long as a teacher can demonstrate that the activity and the related marking criteria logically lead to the stated objective, and that the objective, in turn, logically leads to the fulfillment of a specific curriculum guide goal, then the teacher can justify his or her evaluation.

When presenting a lesson, the teacher must inform the students of the lesson's purpose (i.e., objective) at the very beginning of the lesson.

SAMPLE LESSON PLAN ON ANCIENT EGYPT

Unit Title:	Ancient Egypt
Lesson Title: Culture Time Capsule	**Grade Level:** 6
Goal:	Students will appreciate the similarities and differences of the world's cultures.
Objective:	By the end of class, students will recognize that the contents of the Pharaoh's tomb reflected the values of Ancient Egypt. Students will demonstrate this understanding by creating a time capsule for which they will draw and include 5 objects that they believe represent modern North American Society.
Materials:	Video *Ancient Egypt*; construction paper, scissors, glue, pens

Gaining Student Attention: Ask students, "If you were stranded on a deserted island, what one object would you want to take with you, and why?"

Procedures:

1. Review previous learning.

2. Ask students what one thing they would take to a deserted island.

3. Show film on Ancient Egypt. Ask students to take note of cultural objects important to the people.

4. Discuss film: Relate film content to Ancient Egyptian burial objects. Ask, "What one thing might an Ancient Egyptian have wanted to have on a deserted island? Why?"

5. In groups of 3, students use construction paper to create a modern-day time capsule. Students choose and draw pictures of 5 modern objects they would put in the time capsule to represent North American Society.

6. Have students present and explain their choices to the class. Teacher helps class realize that tomb contents reflect cultural ways and values.

Summary:	Reiterate notion that contents of Ancient Egyptian tomb reflected cultural values.
Evaluation:	By the end of the class, students will develop, write, draw, and verbally express a list of 5 cultural objects that they believe reflect North American cultural values.
Total Time:	40 minutes

A teacher's lesson plan for a Grade 6 class.

At times, there is nothing more disheartening for a teacher than to thoughtfully plan and present a lesson with passion and verve, only to have a student at the end of the lesson blurt out in confusion tinged with a degree of contempt, "What was the point of that?" Yet such a query underscores a fundamental requirement often overlooked by teachers: When presenting a lesson, the teacher must inform the students of the lesson's purpose (i.e., objective) at the very beginning of the lesson. When the teacher honors this basic principle of instruction, the students are able to better grasp the lesson's relevance and to make connections with previous learning. They also are able to perceive more clearly the purpose of the evaluation activity, and to incorporate into the activity the teacher's expectations. Really, it is the teacher at the planning stage of a lesson who should be asking, "What is the point of this?"; in doing so, mistakes will more likely be avoided.

The planning and delivery of instruction must always be documented. See the templates for a Unit Plan (page 36) and Lesson Plan (page 37).

Culminating Activity Not Reflecting Lesson Content

An English teacher was nearing completion of a novel unit. As a culminating activity, she requested students to "take your favorite scene in [the novel] and write your own screenplay. This screenplay will then be acted out in front of the class." The assignment was worth 60 marks and students were to receive marks based on their ability to 1) write a screenplay, 2) act out a scene from the novel, 3) display creativity, and 4) present a well-organized, well-rehearsed play. However, the school principal noted that this concluding activity failed to evaluate the students' understanding of the concepts and skills taught during the unit. Rather, the principal noted, the teacher's activity evaluated skills that were irrelevant to the unit and were not taught in daily lessons. The teacher agreed with the principal's observations and, subsequently, rewrote the assignment so that it addressed more directly the academic concepts discussed in lessons.

Monthly Year Plan

Month: _____   Teacher: _____

Subject/Course: _____   Date: _____

Goals:

1. _____

2. _____

3. _____

4. _____

Objectives:

1. _____

2. _____

3. _____

4. _____

5. _____

6. _____

7. _____

Concepts/Skills

Full Year Plan: side 1

Teacher _____ Date _____

In the white boxes, list the concepts and skills to be taught for each month.

Subject	September	October	November	December	January	February

Full Year Plan: side 2

Subject	March	April	May	June	July	August

Course Goals Checklist

Subject/Course: _____   Term/Semester: _____

Teacher: _____

Course Goals: **Unit/Date**

❏ _____   _____

❏ _____   _____

❏ _____   _____

❏ _____   _____

❏ _____   _____

❏ _____   _____

❏ _____   _____

❏ _____   _____

❏ _____   _____

❏ _____   _____

❏ _____   _____

❏ _____   _____

❏ _____   _____

❏ _____   _____

❏ _____   _____

❏ _____   _____

❏ _____   _____

❏ _____   _____

❏ _____   _____

❏ _____   _____

❏ _____   _____

❏ _____   _____

❏ _____   _____

❏ _____   _____

❏ _____   _____

❏ _____   _____

❏ _____   _____

❏ _____   _____

❏ _____   _____

Unit Plan

Subject/Course: _____   Unit Title: _____

Time Period: _____   Teacher: _____

Goals:

Content Outline:

Objectives:
By the end of the unit, students will be able to

1.

2.

3.

4.

5.

Activities:

Evaluation:

Lesson Plan

Subject: _____   Date: _____

Unit Title: _____   Lesson Number: _____

Lesson Title: _____

Goal: _____

Lesson Objective: _____

_____

Required Materials:

```
┌──────────────────────────────────────────────────────────────────────┐
│                                                                        │
│                                                                        │
│                                                                        │
│                                                                        │
└──────────────────────────────────────────────────────────────────────┘
```

Time Period: _____

Procedures and Activities:

```
┌──────────────────────────────────────────────────────────────────────┐
│                                                                        │
│                                                                        │
│                                                                        │
│                                                                        │
│                                                                        │
│                                                                        │
│                                                                        │
└──────────────────────────────────────────────────────────────────────┘
```

Evaluation:

```
┌──────────────────────────────────────────────────────────────────────┐
│                                                                        │
│                                                                        │
│                                                                        │
│                                                                        │
└──────────────────────────────────────────────────────────────────────┘
```

Comments:

```
┌──────────────────────────────────────────────────────────────────────┐
│                                                                        │
│                                                                        │
│                                                                        │
│                                                                        │
└──────────────────────────────────────────────────────────────────────┘
```

Calculating Student Letter Grades

Manipulating Cut-off Marks

At the beginning of the academic year, a teacher informed her students that they required a year-end score of 85% in the course to receive an A on their report card. However, toward the end of the year, after the students had written the year-end examination, the teacher realized that her grades were too high, with more than half of the class receiving a grade of A. She told the class that, since the final exam was too easy and in order to keep the class average in line with the school-district average, students would now need 90% in the course to receive an A. Numerous complaints from parents and students were lodged and, consequently, the teacher was required to reinstate her cut-off mark of 85%.

At first glance, most teachers would recognize that the teacher in this case erred when she broke the contractual marking agreement that was established with her students. However, as will be seen, the teacher made a more fundamental error in judgment when she compared the results of student achievement.

Norm-referenced vs. Criterion-referenced Grading

Most adults probably would be thrilled if they scored in the top 2% of an international math contest that involved thousands of people from all over the world. However, these same adults would probably shrink in horror and humiliation if they learned that all their fellow contestants were Kindergarten students. Clearly, for a score to have any real meaning, its source of reference must be known. Letter grades are no different. When teachers assign letter grades to students, they may use one of two fundamentally different grading systems—*norm-referenced* and *criterion-referenced*.

Norm-referenced Grading

Norm-referenced grading compares a student's performance with that of other students.

In norm-referenced grading, a student's performance is relative to the performance of the other students in a class or a particular group. This means that a student's letter grade will depend on the relative strength of performance exhibited by the other students. For example, if a student received a final mark of 60% in a course, but his classmates received less than 20%, then this particular student's final grade might be pushed up to an A.

Within this category of grading, one finds evaluation methods that rely on the *bell curve*. A teacher who uses a bell curve (also called a *normal curve*) assigns marks based on what an average student receives. The bell curve has the advan-

A bell curve, or normal curve, distributes scores symmetrically around the score an average student receives.

tage of allowing the teacher to know precisely how many students in any class will receive a particular letter grade, as a set number of students will automatically fall within each letter-grade category (see the Normal Distribution Curve below). With the bell curve, a set, limited number of students must receive an A, some must receive a B, and some must also fail. The largest number of students will cluster around the graph's hump. It is the teacher's task to determine the cut-off marks for the various letter grades.

NORMAL DISTRIBUTION CURVE

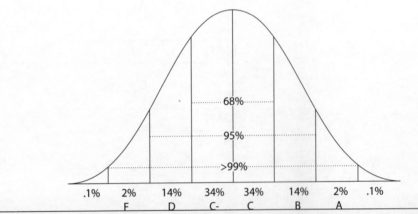

Any set of student scores can be represented using a normal distribution curve. The teacher knows in advance the percentage of students that will fall between the line segments and, consequently, how many students will receive an A, how many will receive a C, and how many will fail. The graph's hump represents the average, or normal score.

NORM-REFERENCED GRADING

In the figure Norm-Referenced Grading, the teacher has decided that only students in the top 10% will receive a first-class mark.

Individual Test Scores		
99 99		top 10% of students receive an A (Number = 2)
98 90 90		15% of students receive a B (Number = 3)
89 89 89 89 86	86 82 81 81 81	50% of students receive a C (Number = 10)
80 80 80		15% of students receive a C- (Number = 3)
79 79		lowest 10% of students receive an F (Number = 2)

A norm-referenced approach to grading for a test worth 100 points. The teacher has determined the cut-off points for assigning grades.

Also under the norm-referenced approach, one finds the *distribution gap* method, which draws gaps or spaces between sets of similar scores (see Distribution Gap Method below). With this evaluation method, naturally occurring gaps in student scores represent cut-off points for each letter grade. The first cut-off line would divide scores worthy of an A from the next grade; the scores before the second gap would rate a B+; and so on. With this method, two potential disadvantages exist for students: gaps are formed by chance and by the achievement differences of students; and it prevents fewer borderline marks, thus making it more difficult for students to argue for a higher mark.

DISTRIBUTION GAP METHOD

99		82		
99	A	81		
98		81		
[GAP]		81	C	
90		80		
90	B	80		
[GAP]		[GAP]		
89		79		
89		79	F	
89	C+			
86				
86				
[GAP]				

The distribution gap method allows the teacher to use arbitrary gaps in student scores to assign grades.

Norm-referenced Grading in Today's Classroom

In today's public schools, norm-referenced evaluation is completely inappropriate for grading student work assigned by the teacher in the classroom. Norm-referenced grading, since it compares a student's work with the abilities of an "average" student, requires a very large group of students in order to have any real meaning, and a meaningful average simply can not be determined satisfactorily from a small population. (For a brief discussion regarding the pitfalls of using norm-referenced standardized tests, see Chapter 5.)

The classroom setting is simply too small to determine a meaningful average, and therefore school districts do not allow norm-referenced grading to be used for teacher-made in-class assignments.

Criterion-referenced Grading

Today's classroom teachers are expected to use a *criterion-referenced* system of evaluation when grading student work. In a criterion-referenced form of evaluation, a student's work is not compared to the work of other students. Rather, as discussed in Chapter 1, a student's assignment receives a mark based on clearly stated criteria, or teacher expectations. This form of grading represents the skills and knowledge a student achieves according to pre-established standards. Under criterion-referenced grading, one finds the commonly used *percentage method*. With the percentage method, a year-end score of 100 percent implies that the student learned all of the material; a score of zero percent implies that the student learned nothing. Percentage scores may be translated into letter grades using cut-off points; for example, 90 percent in a course is an A, 80 percent is a B, and so on.

Criterion-referenced grading assigns marks based on clearly stated criteria or teacher expectations.

Criterion-referenced grading is a double-edged sword. While it may seem transparent enough, it is this very transparency that lulls most teachers into a state of complacency, as they come to accept the notion that cut-off marks in some way reflect true and significant differences in student achievement. In reality, a cut-off point between two letter grades is nothing more than a convenient mechanism to reduce the number of complaints from dissatisfied parents and students. Cut-off points do not reflect true differences in student abilities and they are simply arbitrary demarcations imposed by the teacher, the school, or the school district. A cut-off mark for an A could be set just as easily at 85% as it could at 90%.

In fact, at some point in their career, most teachers quietly make adjustments to cut-off marks, perhaps allowing a student to pass a course that, strictly speaking, the student should have failed. So, what does this mean for teachers? Simply put, since marking often is a subjective endeavor—even with the aid of marking rubrics and criteria—teachers should take care not to be too dogmatic and rigid in their interpretation of student percentage marks. When confronted by a concerned parent or administrator questioning a child's borderline grade, it may be prudent, diplomatic, and—ironically—accurate to recognize the limitations of cut-off marks. As will be seen in Chapter 4, criterion-referenced grading, if it truly is to reflect student achievement, requires that the teacher possess great skill in test construction and marking.

Advantages and Disadvantages of Grading Systems

Criterion-referenced Grading Systems

Advantages

- Most students can achieve a high grade if they work hard and meet the pre-established criteria.
- Final grades reflect a student's mastery of the course goals, and not performance relative to other students.
- Co-operation among students is increased and will not negatively influence individual evaluation.

Disadvantages

- The teacher must determine course standards and criteria for each letter grade and assignment, which may be a problem for new, inexperienced teachers.
- The teacher needs to be aware of the abilities of the students in the class.
- High skill in test preparation is required in order to assess accurately student learning.

Norm-referenced Grading Systems

Advantages

- Student grades can be interpreted by other teachers in the school or district.
- Academically superior students receive high grades.

Disadvantages

- Even though all students may have a solid understanding of the course content, some students in the course must receive a low grade if the other classmates receive high scores.
- Grading standards change from year to year depending on the performance of the students in the class.

> Cut-off points do not reflect true differences in student abilities and are simply arbitrary demarcations imposed by the teacher, the school, or the school district.

How to Determine Report-card Marks

The Percentage Method and Weighting Marks

Not surprisingly, a final grade reflects the scores achieved on individual assignments and tests. However, the student with the highest end-of-year overall mark in a course may not in fact have received the highest scores on assignments. The Sample from a Teacher's Marks Book below displays the term marks for two students. Karen and Bob both have five sets of scores that can be used for evaluation purposes. Looking at their individual scores, one might think that Bob, who did better than Karen on four out of five assignments, will get the better letter grade on his report card. However, this is not necessarily true, because the student who will get the better end-of-year grade is determined by how the teacher *weights* the assignments. Weighting refers to the value or percent of the final mark given to each assignment. Some assignments, regardless of the number of points awarded, are emphasized more heavily than are others when calculating final marks.

A teacher who *weights* assignments according to the pie chart shown in Weighting Assignments: Sample 1 below will place the greatest emphasis on tests (50%) and will give Karen a higher grade than Bob, even though Bob received more points than Karen. Karen will get the higher grade because she did better on the test. However, a different teacher, who may choose to assign grades based on the weights shown in the pie chart in Sample 2 below, would give Bob the higher final grade, since the Tests category is less heavily emphasized.

SAMPLE FROM A TEACHER'S MARKS BOOK

Assignments	Speech	Poster Project	Work-sheet #1	Work-sheet #2	Test	Total Points
Karen	10/20	16/20	6/10	7/10	29/30	68/90
Bob	16/20	18/20	9/10	9/10	20/30	72/90

WEIGHTING ASSIGNMENTS: SAMPLE 1

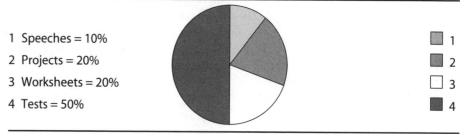

1 Speeches = 10%

2 Projects = 20%

3 Worksheets = 20%

4 Tests = 50%

The category Tests has a weight of 50%.

WEIGHTING ASSIGNMENTS: SAMPLE 2

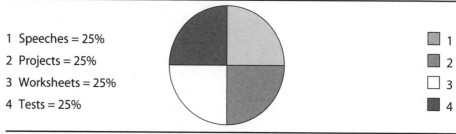

1 Speeches = 25%

2 Projects = 25%

3 Worksheets = 25%

4 Tests = 25%

The category Tests has a weight of 25%.

Calculating and Weighting Course Grades

The process of weighting assignments can be best understood by picturing a student's schoolwork being placed into various containers. Each container would have a different category or label placed on it, and within each container one would find the sum total of all the assignments that fit that container's label. Each container would be assigned a different value, usually a percent. Located below are the marks for an individual student, which have been categorized under four general labels: Speeches, Projects, Worksheets, and Tests.

STUDENT'S NAME: SUSAN GREEN

Category	Speeches (10%)	Projects (20%)	Worksheets (20%)	Tests (50%)
Assignment scores	10/10	16/20	6/10	29/30
	8/10	22/30	7/10	28/30
			2/10	
Total point value	/20	/50	/30	/60

When the teacher calculates a final course grade, the assignments within each category are added together:

Speeches	Projects	Worksheets	Tests
18/20	38/40	15/30	57/60

The teacher then calculates the student's final mark according to the values assigned to each category:

Speeches = 18/20 $\Longrightarrow$ 18/20 x 10% = .09 (9%)

Projects = 38/50 $\Longrightarrow$ 38/50 x 20% = .152 (15.2%)

Worksheets = 15/30 $\Longrightarrow$ 15/30 x 20% = .1 (10%)

Tests = 57/60 $\Longrightarrow$ 57/60 x 50% = .475 (47.5%)

As can be seen from the above calculations, Susan will receive 47.5% out of a possible 50% for her tests; 10% out of a possible 20% for worksheets; 15.2% out of a possible 20% for projects; and 9% out of a possible 10% for her speeches. These scores are added together to obtain the student's course score:

9% + 15.2% +10% + 47.5% = 81.7%

Susan's score of 81.7% would then be used to assign her a letter grade on her report card.

The Total Points Method

The total points method may also be used to calculate report-card grades. This method requires that the teacher assign a certain number of points to an assignment based on its importance. For example, a test that is worth 30% of the final grade would be assigned a value of 30 points out of a possible 100 points (or 60 points out of a possible 200 points, for that matter). At the end of the course, the student's points would be added together as seen in the example below:

Assignment	Points
Quiz	18/20
Term Paper	54/60
Exam	48/50
Lab Assignment #1	38/40
Lab Assignment #2	29/30
Total Points	187/**200**

The student's total points would then be assigned a letter grade using pre-established guidelines:

Total Points	Grade
180–200	A
160–179	B
140–159	C
120–139	D
0–119	Fail

The reality is that many teachers at the beginning of any academic year do not know the number and nature of the assignments they will give to their students. These often are determined as the course progresses. If a teacher were to determine in advance the number and value of assignments to be given to students throughout the year, then that teacher might find teaching flexibility greatly reduced; predetermining assignments would possibly prevent the teacher from addressing the specific needs of students in a particular class. Also, the possibility exists that the teacher could be held legally or professionally accountable should he or she deviate from the stated agenda.

The Value of Converting Letter Grades

An English literature student received an end-of-year report card grade of 84%. He missed receiving an A by only 2%, as the school district required 86% for a first-class mark. Rather than passively accept a B for his efforts, the student reviewed the marks he received on all his previous course assignments and decided to calculate the final mark for himself. He noted that on one of his essay assignments—a group research project—he received a letter grade of A rather than a numerical score. He correctly concluded that this mark of A could in fact represent a wide numerical range of anywhere between 86% and 100%. As a result, it was difficult for this student to accurately calculate his overall percent; possibly requiring the teacher to increase his overall grade.

A letter grade can represent a wide value range, and this is why it is so important for a teacher using letter grades for individual assignments to convert the letter grade into a numerical score. In this way, a student or parent can better calculate a course grade for himself and the teacher can be more accurate and precise in reporting grades. Furthermore, this case highlights the danger inherent in assigning a single mark to a group of students for collaborative projects and assignments.

The Problem with a Shared Group Mark

Teacher W assigned students a group research project, which required students jointly to create one visual poster that detailed the major events that led to the beginning of World War I. Shortly afterwards, Teacher W received a phone call from an anxious parent who expressed her concern that her daughter's project mark was going to be negatively influenced by the academic incompetence of the other group members. This parent further asserted that she would not allow her child's ambition of going to university to be threatened by the poor work ethic of her peers.

Often teachers will assign projects that require collaboration between students for reasons of limited resources, issues of sociality, and the convenience of a reduced marking load. While group activities can be used to promote learning, from an educational research perspective it is difficult for a teacher to justify the practice of giving one mark to an entire group for a single assignment. Rather, a teacher should divide the assignment into smaller tasks and award marks based on each student's successful completion of those tasks. In this way, a student's grade will not be lowered due to the inabilities of other group members, and parents will less likely feel the need to question the accuracy of a teacher's mark. A student's report-card grade must reflect the achievement of only that particular individual.

Ten Strategies to Ensure Accuracy

1. Clearly state whether or not an assignment will be recorded and used for calculating a course grade. A teacher can assign work for a variety of non-evaluative purposes, such as classroom management, discipline, student motivation, and monitoring student progress. However, a student must be informed when the work is first given that the assignment is or is not going to be used to calculate a report-card letter grade.

2. Make sure that each assignment is designated clearly to an established marking category. Students must be informed what marking category the assignment belongs to. Students and parents do not always recognize that the teacher may categorize an assignment differently than they themselves might. Also, the different category labels and their values must be stated to the students at the beginning of the year. Once the weights have been set, a teacher can not change them to his or her advantage.

The "Mis-categorized" Assignment

A science teacher marked all course work using four broad categories, and allotted marks accordingly: lab reports (30%), projects (10%), worksheets (10%), and tests (50%). The teacher gave the class a take-home assignment. The teacher classified this assignment as a lab report, whereas the students and parents believed it was a project. Clearly, the way in which the assignment was categorized would change the weight and value assigned to it and would influence a student's final report card grade. After discussing the matter with the principal, the teacher agreed that the category to which the assignment belonged was not clearly stated. Consequently, he allowed the students to write another assignment for extra credit if they wished.

3. Check if there are departmental weights to follow. Often, weights are determined at the departmental level, which means that all the teachers teaching the same course will use the same values for assignment categories. This might mean, for example, that all math teachers would agree that tests are worth 50% in a particular course.

4. Make sure a final report-card letter grade is not derived from only one assessment method or assignment category. Over the years, research has shown that students do not all learn in the same way and that different students have different learning styles. This means that different students may excel with one method of evaluation rather than another. Likewise, a teacher should not allow any one in-class evaluation activity to skew a student's comprehensive mark to the detriment of all other activities.

Too Much Emphasis on One Test

A history teacher based 50% of his course marks on tests and the other 50% on assignments. On the first day of class, the students were informed of this weighting. The teacher based the year's first report-card grade on one test and seven assignments. One particular student received 88% on all seven assignments, but 45% (Fail) on the one test. She complained to the teacher that the one test, since it was 50% of her grade, skewed her mark and that, consequently, her letter grade did not represent her understanding of the concepts. She claimed that it was unfair that the one test should have the same value as the other seven assignments. The student informed the principal of the situation and, after investigating the matter, the principal concluded that the one test was not more accurate in assessing the student's understanding of the course goals than the seven assignments. The principal also noted that the assignments dated back over several months, took the student many hours to complete, and covered the same specific goals as did the test. The teacher was required to increase the number of tests given to students in order to more closely match the number of points allotted to student assignments and to account for potential test bias.

In order to fairly assess all students and to give all students a chance to show what they have learned to the best of their ability, teachers should evaluate students using a variety of methods.

Test Anxiety and Evaluation Methods

A Grade 10 student complained to the principal that his history teacher based all student letter grades on in-class tests. The student noted that he experienced a great deal of nervousness and anxiety when he wrote tests and that, therefore, he was unable to demonstrate his true understanding of the course goals. The principal was informed of the student's concerns and, in an interview with the teacher, noted that the teacher failed to use a variety of methods to evaluate student learning, and did not take into account the great variety of student learning styles that existed in his class. The principal also noted that no one learning style or evaluation method necessarily is better than any other. The principal went on to note that great care must be taken when evaluating children and adolescents, because they still are growing intellectually and lack the psychological maturity of adults. Subsequently,

Variety in evaluation methods is especially important for younger age groups since they are developmentally less mature and may lack specific and necessary study skills.

the student was assessed using written essays and worksheets in conjunction with formal classroom tests.

5. Provide occasional updates regarding grades. There should be no surprises when a student receives a report card. Throughout the year, a student or parent should know the student's current standing and what needs to be done to improve his or her grade. Throughout the year, prior to distributing report cards, the teacher should review the marks with each student; missing assignments and possible marking errors may become more readily apparent.

6. Make sure that a disproportionate value has not been given to any one assignment. A teacher may give an assignment a value of 100 points when it could have, or should have, been marked out of a possible 10 points. Some teachers will give a high value to an assignment in an attempt to make the assignment seem important and impressive; indeed, students tend to take more seriously an assignment that is more heavily weighted. However, the teacher must display consistency in the values given to each assignment. If some assignments are worth significantly more marks than others, then the teacher must be able to justify the given values using the same factors for determining percentage weights.

The teacher should keep accurate records of student work that is late, incomplete, or plagiarized. Use Student Marks: Anecdotal on page 49.

7. In the marks book, indicate the students who submit work that is incomplete or late. While this suggestion may seem obvious, many teachers have found themselves on the defensive when students or parents accuse them of having lost student work. The teacher who asks students at the beginning of the class to drop completed homework into the marking box without recording their names is a naïve individual who is playing a game of Russian roulette with his or her reputation; the odds are good that at some point students will take advantage of the teacher's trusting attitude and pretend to have completed and submitted an assignment when they did not. To help prevent being falsely accused of losing student work, teachers are advised to approach each student's desk with marks book in hand and, one by one, collect each student's work. Students who fail to turn in their work should have this information recorded beside their names. Likewise, students who turn in work late or incomplete should have this information documented for future reference.

8. Verify all individual assignment and test marks with each individual student before calculating a final report-card grade. By verbally reviewing with students the marks they have received for each assignment, possible errors and discrepancies may be recognized and corrected.

9. For each reporting period, make sure that a report-card letter grade is accompanied by a numerical value. Typically, a school district will issue report cards to students several times throughout the academic year. Some schools, in order to determine a final year-end grade, will average out the letter grades received in each reporting period for the academic year. Therefore, in order to verify a student's final year-end mark, the teacher must know a student's specific numerical score for each reporting period. Simply knowing the letter grade for each term is insufficient.

10. Do not publicly post marks and grades. When possible, the list of class marks should remain in the hands of the teacher or administrator. On numerous occasions, parents have been known to obtain a class list of marks issued by an individual teacher and used them to the detriment of that classroom teacher.

Posting a List of Class Marks

As was common practice at her school, a science teacher posted on the school wall the scores that her students received on the final examination. One student took this list of marks and shared it with his parents. The boy's parents in turn, took the list to the school-district superintendent and claimed that the large number of students with low scores on the list was evidence of the teacher's incompetence. While the teacher was eventually exonerated, for many months she had to endure numerous district administrators coming into her class to evaluate her teaching performance, and was the topic of rumor and gossip in the community.

The Role of Effort

"But I worked so hard on it!" is a common defence used by students when arguing with the teacher for a higher mark on an assignment. However, students and parents often fail to realize that student effort can not legitimately be used as a factor when seeking a higher mark from the teacher. Likewise, a teacher can not use a lack of student effort to justify a grade. Effort—the amount of time and energy a student puts into an assignment—is highly subjective and difficult for a teacher to measure. Also, a student's level of effort usually does not reflect the requirements of the course goals. A teacher who wishes to include student effort in a report card can do so only as a work habit comment. (*Good*, *Satisfactory*, and *Needs Improvement* are common work effort descriptors found on report cards.)

Student Marks: Anecdotal

Student's Name	Mark	Comment	Mark	Comment	Mark	Comment	Mark	Comment	Mark	Comment	Total

Comments: **L** = Late   **NE** = No Effort   **A** = Absent
I = Incomplete   **GE** = Good Effort   **T** = Tardy
NS = Not Submitted   **P** = Plagiarized   **Ch** = Cheated

Constructing Valid Tests

A Mismatch between Test and Instruction

A student-teacher in a physics class taught all lessons for one of her units at the knowledge level, and during in-class activities required students only to recognize and recall facts and rules. However, in her unit test, which she had hastily created the night before, many of her questions required students to solve questions that were at the higher levels of application and analysis. The supervising teacher informed her that she was unable to give test questions at the analysis level when all the student activities in her lessons had been at the knowledge level. She was informed that the test questions had to meet the level of thought stated in her objectives and presented in her lessons. She was required to omit those test questions that tested beyond the knowledge level and to adjust the students' scores.

Too often, teachers will inform their students what topics will be on a test but not what they will have to do with those topics. Tests are meant to evaluate course goals. Therefore, on any test, it is not enough that a student knows what content and topics will be evaluated; rather, the student also must know what goals and objectives will be tested.

Good test construction involves more than just asking students tough questions. Ironically, despite the high premium placed on student test scores, many teachers do not receive adequate formal training in test design and construction. Test construction is actually a highly skilled endeavor that requires patience and subtlety of technique, if the test is to measure what it purports to measure. The simple truth is that not all teacher-made tests are created equal—some are good, and many are poor. When teachers fail to recognize a poorly constructed test question, they leave open to criticism their evaluation methods.

As discussed in Chapter 1, an assignment given to a student can be categorized and assigned to one of six cognitive levels of thought, based on the verb used to frame the assignment. Similarly, test questions also may require students to perform at various cognitive levels. In this sample psychology test question, the specific goal being tested is at the knowledge level since the action word is *identify*, which requires students only to recall facts.

Unit Goal: Students will be able to *identify* different types of phobias.
Test Question: Which of the following is NOT a type of phobia?
   a) agoraphobia
   b) claustrophobia
   c) acrophobia
   d) bipolar disorder

A test question is said to be *valid*, or acceptable, when the test's questions accurately measure the student's comprehension of the course goals. As seen in A Mismatch between Test and Instruction (above), a test is *invalid*, or unacceptable, when the test questions do not accurately measure what they are supposed to measure. For example, a teacher's unit on electricity may have the following unit objective: "Students will be able to *state* Ohm's law." Since this goal requires students to state a law, it requires students to perform at the knowledge level of thought. However, let us imagine that the teacher asks the class on the unit test to apply their knowledge to a new setting. The test question might ask students to "*Compute* what happens to electrical voltage if resistance is decreased while amperage remains constant." Clearly, this test question would be invalid (or unacceptable) because it does not measure the stated specific goal. The question has not measured what it should measure since it requires students to perform a task that goes beyond the stated specific goal. Rather than measuring the students' understanding of the stated specific goal (that is to say, "stating Ohm's Law") the students are asked to perform a task that is not related to the goal (i.e., to compute).

Before writing any test, students should be informed what course goals and objectives are going to be tested. With this information, students will understand the purpose of the test question and will understand better the teacher's expectations. In fact, students will often change the way they study for a test depending on the nature of the goal or objective being evaluated.

The Table of Specifications

Prior to constructing the test questions, and to help ensure that the test is a valid measurement of student learning, a teacher should first create a test blueprint, called a *table of specifications*. For the teacher, it serves three purposes:

- it allows the teacher to make sure that the test covers all the class topics
- it helps to ensure that the test covers all of the unit objectives
- it helps to ensure that the questions on the test reflect the amount of class time spent teaching the concepts.

The Completed Table of Specifications on page 52 is for a biology unit test on the structures of the brain. In the left-hand column, the teacher writes the content topics to be covered on the test. In the example provided, these topics are *the cerebellum, the medulla, the thalamus, the corpus callosum, the cerebrum,* and *the pons,* which are all parts of the brain. Next, along the top of the table, the teacher writes the specific goals that will be tested. These specific goals are the behaviors and learning that the student must show on the test: *knows basic function, knows early researchers, can compare and contrast systems.* The column on the right-hand side is used to indicate the number of total items in that row. The first two specific goals along the top of the table require the student to perform at the knowledge level of thought. This is true since the action verb used is "know." The third specific goal is at the evaluation level since it uses the verbs "compare and contrast." The next step is for the teacher to create test questions that can be categorized within each box or cell. For example, a question that requires a student to know the basic function of the cerebellum would be indicated in the corresponding empty cell in the upper left corner. As can be seen, the first topic—the cerebellum—will have seven related topics on the test, three of which will ask students to compare and contrast. Also, it is evident that this exam will have twelve questions that test the specific goal "knows basic functions." In total, this test will have thirty-six questions.

If an examination question does not assess course goals and objectives, or goes beyond them, then the question lacks validity, and the student and parent may have grounds for demanding that the question be removed from the examination.

The Table of Specifications on page 62 can be used by the teacher to plan test construction.

COMPLETED TABLE OF SPECIFICATIONS

Specific Goals

Test Content	Knows basic function	Knows early researchers	Compare and contrast systems	Total Items
Cerebellum	2	2	3	**7**
Medulla	2	2	2	**6**
Thalamus	3	2	2	**7**
Corpus Callosum	2	2	2	**6**
Cerebrum	1	1	2	**4**
Pons	2	2	2	**6**
Total Items	**12**	**11**	**13**	**36**

The specific goals, or objectives, are indicated on the top row.

TEACHER TIPS

• **Provide students with a copy of the table of specifications before they write the test.** Many teachers will share a copy of their table of specifications with their students, as it can serve as an excellent guide for studying. The table will inform test-takers not only what content they will need to know, but also what they will have to do with that material. Some teachers will also inform students of the exact number of questions in each cell. This can help students manage studying time, and puts increased responsibility for learning in the hands of students. A table of specifications often can be obtained for standardized and district-wide tests by directly contacting the test's publisher.

• **Use instructional time to calculate the number of questions that should fall within each cell.** Some goals are considered more important than others; therefore, the teacher will spend more class time addressing them. This means that class instructional time may be used as an indicator of the topic's importance and the number of related questions that should appear on a test. For example, if one math-class hour is spent on the topic "measuring angles" in a five-hour unit on angles, then a proportionate number of related questions should appear on the test:

$$\frac{1 \text{ hour}}{5 \text{ hours}} = .20 \text{ or } 20\%$$

Therefore, if the test has ten questions, it would be reasonable to assume that two of these questions will deal with measuring angles. It would be unacceptable, if not dishonest, for a teacher to spend 90% of class time teaching toward a set of objectives and later, on a test, to devote only 10% of the questions to these objectives. (Of course, teachers often find themselves having to spend a great deal of time re-teaching a particular concept, not because it is necessarily important, but because the students simply do not understand it.)

• **Subject each test question to an item analysis.** If the same examination is to be used with classes in the future, possibly invalid or problematic test questions can be rooted out by determining which questions had disproportionately high or low correct responses. By weeding out these questions, the test may provide a more accurate measurement of student learning.

It is possible for parents, students, and administrators to have specific questions omitted from a teacher's test, and even to have tests rewritten by examinees, if it can be shown that the test questions or method of scoring is invalid. Parents and students may contest individual questions on an examination in the hopes of increasing a student's overall raw test score. For this reason, teachers must take care to design individual test items that can hold up against scrutiny.

Essay Tests

Essay tests may require students to provide a lengthy written response ranging from only a paragraph to several pages. Teachers will often use an essay-style test for the following reasons:

- Essay tests are easy to create and take little time to develop.
- Essay tests allow the teacher to see the thinking process used by the student.
- Essay tests allow the teacher to measure higher levels of thought (analysis, synthesis, and evaluation).

However, essay tests do have some disadvantages for both the teacher and the student:

- They allow the student to demonstrate his or her learning and knowledge in only a few limited areas; consequently, they do not allow the student to demonstrate all that he or she knows. Rather, students must be thoroughly familiar with the details of only one or two topics.
- These tests can take a long time for the teacher to read and mark.
- They are not objectively marked and, therefore, different teachers will often assign different scores to the same test papers.
- They require that the student be able to write well and be able to express thoughts on paper. This is a disadvantage for those students who have trouble writing essays and who are not native English speakers.

Clarity of Test Language

Brian, whose first language is Korean, was enrolled in a biology class. Brian's family had left Korea when he was six years old and, immersed in an English-speaking environment for nearly a decade, Brian's conversational English was fluent. After the first semester of studies in biology, Brian received an A on his report card. Unfortunately, in the second semester of this course, he wrote and failed an essay examination. He complained to the teacher that he failed the test not because he had trouble with the biology concepts, but because he could not understand the sophisticated sentence patterns and vocabulary words that the teacher had used to phrase the question. The teacher informed Brian that if this were the case, he should have brought it to his attention during the examination. Since he had not done so, he would have to accept the failing grade.

Even experienced teachers incorrectly assume that students know the meaning of specific words. Tests in biology and math, for example, should measure a student's reading ability only when it leads to the stated course goals.

The teacher's counter-argument in the above case—essentially, "You should have told me so before"—is commonly used by teachers in an attempt to justify their marking decisions. Yet, such a defence is mere rhetoric. The teacher is the trained educational professional, whose duty is to ensure the fair and accurate evaluation of his diverse learners. Students, by their very nature, lack the experience and cognitive maturity to recognize their own intellectual limitations and shortcomings, and therefore have difficulty gauging how well they can handle a test or assignment when it is first presented. In Brian's case, the principal who mediated the situation concluded that the reading level required by the student to answer the question was well above the student's grade-level ability; consequently, the skills being measured were clouded by an irrelevant variable.

• **The test question must be written in a way so that everyone who reads it will understand exactly what is being asked.** There should be only one interpretation of the question. If the question does not have a clearly defined problem, then it is difficult for the teacher to mark and to score the great variety of possibly correct test answers that will be turned in. This also means that a statement of conditions should be present.

• **If an essay examination has several essay questions to answer, the teacher must state the weight or value of each question.** Many examinations require the student to answer more than one essay question; however, not all questions may be assigned the same value by the marker. A student who knows the specific value of each essay question is better able to budget the time spent answering each question.

• **If an essay examination allows the student to select his or her own question to answer, the teacher must use the same marking criteria for all questions.** Some tests provide students with a selection of questions from which the student may choose. When a student is given the opportunity to select the question, the mark received by the student may at times reflect the teacher's own preference for a particular question. Thus, a teacher must be careful to ensure that a student's test mark reflects that student's comprehension of the content and not the student's choice of question. This problem can be minimized if the teacher is looking for and evaluating the same concepts or skills in all of the questions.

Marking Essay Tests

Some teachers find it difficult to justify and defend the mark they have given to a student's essay test. Since answers on essay tests often lack the preciseness of being either simply right or wrong, but tend to have degrees or shades of correctness, marking consistency among teachers can be quite low when compared to marking of so-called objective formats, such as multiple-choice tests.

The Point-Score Method

In the *point-score* method, the teacher marks the essay using a teacher-made template of the desired response. The teacher writes his own ideal answer and then assigns a value to each important fact or detail in the answer. Points, or marks, are given to the student when his or her test answer includes specific details found in the teacher's ideal answer. The Point-Score Method below shows the answers a student should include in his written response in order to receive a possible 25 marks.

POINT-SCORE METHOD

Test Question

In a 300-word essay, discuss how Geoffrey Chaucer uses figures of speech in the *Canterbury Tales*. Be sure to give examples from three of his tales.

Scoring the student's answer:

Student mentions three tales	5 points
Student discusses metaphor	5 points
Student discusses similes	5 points
Student discusses puns	5 points
Student uses proper essay structure	5 points
Total	25 points

This method requires the teacher to list the key features required in a student's response.

Two teachers marking the same essay test may score the same student response quite differently from one another and it is this marking imprecision that can shake the confidence of parents, students, and administrators.

The Point-Score Evaluation template on page 63 should be completed by the teacher prior to marking a student's paragraph or essay test response. Student work is compared to the stated criteria listed under *Required Student Responses* and marks should be allotted accordingly.

The Rubric Method

With the *rubric method* of marking essay tests, the teacher assigns a score to the student's test answer based on the overall quality. This method differs from the point-score method in that it does not give points to the student every time an answer includes the same information as the teacher's ideal answer. A teacher using a marking rubric (see Chapter 1) does not assign values or marks to specific comments made by the student. Rather, a rubric is similar to a sliding scale, as it measures the same criteria, or variables, for each letter grade. In the Detailed Marking Rubric on page 7, one can see that it is not the amount of information that is being measured, but the student's level of ability in relation to the same set of skills. All the letter-grade levels across the rubric measure the same skills and abilities.

The Sorting Method

A classic, but hackneyed joke teachers use to entertain and torment their students goes something like this: "How will I mark your essays, you ask? Tonight, when I go home, I will throw them down my basement stairs. The ones that land the farthest must have more pages and, therefore, will get an A. Those that land the closest to me must be the lightest, and therefore, will exhibit the least amount of work, and will get an F." This trite attempt at humor can be made only by a teacher who has strength of conviction that his true and practised marking methods are sound, justifiable, and transparent. In the real world, it would be difficult for a teacher to evaluate an essay's worth based on its literal and relative weight. And yet, with the *sorting method*, it is the relative worth that is weighed. This seldom-used method of evaluation requires the teacher to review briefly all the test papers and to sort them into three stacks based on the quality of the student's written answers. The best papers go into one stack, the average papers go into a second stack, and the worst papers go into a third stack. The papers then are read more carefully a second time, and each stack is then divided into even smaller stacks. Letter grades are then assigned to each stack.

Of course, these days, most teachers will not use this grading method for several reasons:

- it is difficult for the teacher to explain why a test paper was assigned to a particular stack and to justify the mark it received.
- it is a form of norm-referenced evaluation, which may not be practised in today's classrooms.
- it is especially difficult for young and inexperienced teachers to use, since they have not seen enough sample test answers in their short careers to make comparative judgments and assign tests to appropriate stacks.

> **Whether a teacher uses the point-score method or the rubric method to mark student essay tests, the teacher must be able to justify and explain a student's test score results.**

TEACHER TIPS

• **Before students write any essay test, the teacher must inform them how the answer will be marked.** The teacher must tell the students if he will be using the point-score method or a marking rubric.

• **If a marking rubric is to be used, then the students must know the skills, knowledge, and level of performance required in order to receive an A.** It is suggested that the teacher give a copy of the rubric to his or her students. Having a copy of the rubric will in no way give away the details of the answer as it will only inform the students what level of performance will be required for each letter grade. This also requires that the language of the rubric be age-appropriate.

• **A student should be given the higher of the two marks should two markers disagree.** Scoring essay tests is highly unreliable, and so it is common for an essay test to be marked

The Team Evaluation Report on page 64 should be used when a student's work is evaluated by multiple teachers. After reading the assignment, each teacher provides a written comment and a mark. The highest mark should be awarded to the student and indicated in the box in the upper right-hand corner.

Many school districts do not allow the practice of student marking, due in part to issues of student confidentiality, and insist that the teacher assume full responsibility for marking tests and assignments.

by a team of markers. Often, when a test answer receives two different scores from two different markers, the final score will be an average between the two marks. This means that if one marker gives a test answer a mark of 74 and a second marker gives the same answer a mark of 80, then the middle score of 77 will be awarded to the student. However, the practice of averaging grades is invalid and unacceptable. Taking an average is simply an expedient and convenient way for two markers to resolve differences and to reach a common "middle ground"; however, it does not reflect student ability. The problem with averaging the scores of test markers becomes apparent when an extreme case is examined: a test paper receives 40% from one marker and 70% from a second marker giving it an average score of 55%. Clearly, a score of 55% does a disservice to the student, for the exam paper is either at the C+ (70%) level or it is not. Reducing the student's score to a bare pass (55%) does not accurately reflect the student's comprehension of the course goals. Rather, the higher of the two marks should be given to the student.

• **In order to increase marking consistency among teachers, joint practice marking sessions should be held.** When marking an English exam, for example, two teachers may both agree with the rubric that an A requires the student to write a thesis statement that is "clear and interesting," but they may disagree on what that looks like—"clear and interesting" likely means different things to different teachers. By meeting as a group and grading sample essays, individual teachers can discuss their marking differences and better reach a consensus and marking unanimity.

• **Provide students with sample work that illustrates each letter-grade category.** In this way, the student will have concrete models to follow and will better understand the differences between first- and second-class work.

• **Be especially cautious of having students mark tests and assignments.** Having students mark each other's work can save the teacher hours of marking; however, it can pose problems for students, due to a lack of student motivation and marking inexperience. Even objective tests, such as a multiple-choice test, are not free from student marking errors. If a teacher does have students mark in-class tests, then the teacher should repeat the correct answers once the marked test has been returned to students, so the students can check the accuracy of their own test scores. Tests that require the student to give a so-called subjective answer, such as stating a personal opinion or defending an argument or point-of-view, should never be marked by students.

Multiple-Choice Tests

Most students seem greatly to prefer multiple-choice tests to essay tests, perhaps because they think that they have a better chance of passing when the answer is located somewhere in front of them. A multiple-choice question has two parts: a question or problem (called a *stem*) and three or four possible answers (called *alternatives*). The student is asked to pick the one alternative that best completes the statement or answers the question. The possible answers that are not correct are called *distracters*, since they are designed to provide a distraction from the correct answer. The format of a typical multiple-choice question can be seen here:

Question: Which of the following animals has wings and can fly?
Alternatives: a) a dog
                b) a cat
                c) a penguin
                d) an eagle

A teacher will use a multiple-choice test format for the following reasons:

- It can be marked quickly by the teacher or using a scoring machine.
- It can be marked objectively, since an answer is considered either right or wrong based on the alternative choices.
- It allows the teacher to ask many questions and to test a wide sample of content or goals.
- It allows other teachers marking the test to get the same result.
- Its structure tends to reduce student complaints regarding test scores, since possible responses are limited.

However, multiple-choice tests do have some disadvantages for both the teacher and the student:

- They take a long time for the teacher to create (although many teachers will use the same tests year after year).
- Since it is more difficult for a teacher to write multiple-choice test questions that operate at the higher levels of thought, these tests frequently require students simply to recall facts, and prevent them from demonstrating their creativity and originality.
- Multiple-choice tests favor students who can read well.

Testing the Validity of Multiple-choice Questions

In order for a multiple-choice question to be valid, one must be able to answer the following questions affirmatively:

1. Does the question, or stem, have a clear problem to solve? Here is an invalid test question:

Question: Cats…
a) are domesticated animals.
b) have nine lives.
c) are related to lions.
d) purr when they are happy.

What exactly is being tested in this question? Is the student expected to know the history, the biology, the mythology, or the social behavior of cats? Even experts on the subject would probably disagree as to the correct answer. The purpose of the question must be clear.

2. Does the question have only one correct answer? This condition may seem obvious, but even expert teachers may inadvertently fail to recognize that a question may be read in more than one context. In the question below, the teacher intended the correct answer to be *d) thinking*:

Question: Which one of the following does NOT belong with the others?
a) dog
b) cat
c) Jupiter
d) thinking

The intended answer, *thinking*, is a verb while the other three alternatives are nouns. However, a student could successfully argue that *c) Jupiter* is also correct, since it is an inanimate object incapable of possessing cognition. One way teachers can minimize the chances of students successfully arguing that a second, but possibly correct, answer exists among the distracters is by stating in the directions that students must "identify the one best answer." Of course, "the best" is most often a value judgment based on personal preference and opinion. If a dispute should arise regarding the best answer, several other knowledgeable teachers may be required to weigh in on the debate.

3. Is proper grammar used by the teacher? So as not to confuse the student, alternative answers must be grammatically consistent with the stem. In the example below, the answer (*has 6 legs*) would be invalid since the grammar used in the answer does not match the stem (*has* should be *have*):

Question: According to the course textbook, spiders…
a) has 6 legs
b) have 8 legs
c) have backbones

4. Is the question free from racial stereotypes and biases? Research shows that a student's performance on a test will suffer when test questions portray that student's racial or cultural group in negative or stereotypical ways. For example, a teacher would possibly put some Asian students at a disadvantage if he were to ask a math question that relied on the old stereotype that all Asians own laundering businesses:

Jimmy Chow owns a laundering business. He receives 10 cents for every shirt that he washes and 25 cents for every collar that he starches. How much money will he make in one day if he washes 12 shirts and starches 7 collars?

Likewise, questions that could be interpreted as possibly poking fun at or stereotyping people with physical disabilities may disrupt the performance of students who themselves have disabilities. In such cases, a student with disabilities could demand that the question be removed from the test should that student have trouble obtaining the correct answer.

5. Does the question recognize that not all cultural groups share the same knowledge and experiences? Today's schools have a multicultural setting; therefore, it is inappropriate for tests or assignments to be biased in favor of one cultural group or social class. For example, students whose cultural backgrounds have not exposed them to a teacup and saucer may lack the necessary cultural knowledge needed to answer the following question: "If Jim has seven tea cups and two bottles of coke, how many saucers will he need?" Indeed, research shows that teachers will often award more points to test questions that rely on answers that revolve around the social middle class.

6. Are trickery and deceit absent? A teacher who uses so-called trick questions on a test is not measuring a student's understanding of the course content. The two questions below are problematic:

Question 1: How many animals did Moses bring on his ship?
a) 10
b) 20
c) 100

Question 2: Which of the following is the heaviest?
a) a ton of wheat
b) a ton of gold
c) a ton of feathers

The first question is misleading because it was the biblical character Noah, and not Moses, who built the ark. One must question what curriculum goal the teacher is trying to measure by asking this question. The only thing such a question is testing is the student's ability to detect deception, which, of course, is not a goal in any curriculum guide. In the second question, there is no correct answer, since a ton always weighs the same amount regardless of the material being weighed. This question is invalid simply because no appropriate answer exists among the possible alternatives.

7. Is the stem phrased positively? Negatives, such as *not*, should be avoided in the stem, especially if the alternatives are phrased in the negative. Negatively phrased tasks may become exercises in logic, possibly confusing students and clouding the behavior being measured:

Question: Which statement is not true?
a) 2 + 2 does not equal 4
b) 2 + 3 does not equal 6
c) 1 + 2 does equal 3

Even though the math concept being evaluated here is at a primary level, the question is hardly a fair one to ask young students. Also, if the word *not* is used in the stem, then it should be brought to the student's attention by using bold or capital letters.

True/False Tests

In the minds of most students, the only test better than a multiple-choice test is a true/false test since examinees are pretty well guaranteed to achieve a score of 50%. These tests present the student with a statement to which the student must agree or disagree using the statements *true* or *false.* Generally speaking, teachers use a true/false test format because

- it does not take a lot of time to develop.
- it allows all students of all abilities the chance to receive a passing score.

Interestingly, teachers tend to have the answers to the majority of true/false test questions be "false." The reasoning behind this is simple: people have a natural tendency to agree rather than disagree. (If you doubt this to be true, try running around disagreeing with everyone you meet and see how many friends you can make—and lose!) As a result, students will tend to answer "true" when they do not know an answer. Here lies the basic problem with this so-called objective test: a student who correctly responds with "false" to a stem is not displaying evidence that he or she knows the correct answer. Clearly then, as an evaluative tool, the true/false test format is not the most reliable method.

• **The statement must be unequivocally either true or false.** The use of qualifiers, such as *may* or *possibly*, tend to allow the student to find exceptions to the intended response.

Question: A cat *always* has a tail.   T   F

While the teacher's intended answer is *T* (true), undoubtedly there will be some observant child who will recall a cat that had met with some unfortunate accident, or who has met a cat of the Manx breed, which are tailless.

• **The stem should have a clear context or source of reference to guide students.** Stems that require students merely to respond to an opinion or belief are value laden and lack a context. It is more defensible for the teacher to anchor the stem to some stated specific text or organization.

• **The stem should contain only one central idea that requires a student response.** The second question shown is structurally better than the first simply because some students may assume—perhaps correctly—that the italicized part is the teacher's main proposition:

Question 1: Trees, *which are important to animals*, have branches.   T   F

Question 2: In the novel, *Treeland*, trees have branches.   T   F

Fill-in-the-Blank Tests

Another type of objective test is the fill-in-the-blank test (also called the completion test). This form of evaluation seems to remind teachers of the old *Match Game* TV show, in which contestants had to write words in blank spaces in a sentence, usually with humorous consequences. However, unlike the game show, it is imperative that the blank space in a completion test item represents only a key word; when it does not, the test will likely measure the student's reading ability and not knowledge of the course content. For example, in order to complete the statement below, in which non-key words have been omitted, the student needs to be familiar with the rules of grammar:

Matrilocal residence _____ when _____ man lives _____ his wife.

A better completion test item would be as follows:

When a man lives with his wife's family, it is called _____ residence. (Answer: matrilocal)

Matching-Items Tests

Evaluating Short-term Memory

A teacher evaluated his students' comprehension of the course objectives using a matching-items test format. During this two-hour comprehensive examination, students were required to connect 120 individual items in a list to their appropriate stem in order to make a correct statement. The student failure rate for this test was close to 40 percent.

With the matching-items test format, students are presented with a list of stems on one side of the page and a list of possible alternatives on the other half. The students must then match, or connect, each alternative to the proper stem. While many of the conditions necessary for constructing a multiple-choice test apply to the matching-items test, the teacher should also ensure that only a small number of questions or stems—no more than 10 to 15—be used. In this way, the threat of measuring an irrelevant variable, such as search time, will be minimized. All stems and matching items should appear on the same page, so that students do not waste time flipping back and forth while simultaneously trying to recall the items on the previous page. Finally, to facilitate student reading, the test items should proceed from left to right, with the stems on the left-hand side of the page and the responses on the right.

Open-Book Tests

More often than not, the open-book test seems to assume the characteristics of a school urban legend, a myth that offers to students the illusive promise of almost-certain academic success. True to the form of an urban legend, every student seems to know a friend of a friend who once reaped the benefits of such a test, but who themselves never had the opportunity to experience it first-hand. And there is a good reason for this—teachers recognize the questionable evaluative worth of allowing students access to their textbooks and notes during an exam:

- since students mistakenly assume that they will be able to locate answers quickly in their textbooks, they tend to lose their motivation to study.
- tests usually require students to go beyond the simple regurgitation of facts, and instead, require the evaluation and application of content.
- students often waste time simply trying to locate the relevant information. This is especially true in introductory courses in which students typically lack basic knowledge on the subject.

Table of Specifications

SPECIFIC GOALS

Test Content	Objective 1	Objective 2	Objective 3	Objective 4	Total Items
Total Items					

Point-Score Evaluation

Unit: _____   Course/Subject: _____

Teacher: _____

Date: _____

Question: _____

_____

_____

_____

Required Student Responses: Value

- _____   _____

- _____   _____

- _____   _____

- _____   _____

- _____   _____

- _____

                                                    Total

Team Evaluation Report

(Use this form when there are multiple markers for the same student essay or paragraph response.)

Student Name _____

Student Number _____

Subject/Course _____

Question No. _____

Student Score

Evaluator: _____

Student Score: _____

Comments:

_____

_____

_____

_____

Evaluator: _____

Student Score: _____

Comments:

_____

_____

_____

_____

Evaluator: _____

Student Score: _____

Comments:

_____

_____

_____

_____

5

Standardized Tests

Parents and students often mistakenly believe that high or superior test scores achieved by students on a teacher-made test reflect superior teaching (or more likely, superior student ability), and that low-test scores reflect poor instruction or student inability. The reality is that teachers can and do construct "easy" tests when they want to raise student scores, or create difficult tests when they want to lower the class average. In an effort to minimize marking inconsistency and the potential for bias that is associated with teacher-made tests and evaluation methods, educators, school districts, government agencies, and various academic institutions may evaluate students using standardized tests. Standardized tests may be designed to evaluate a student's academic skills and abilities, to test a student's aptitude or likelihood of success in future academic programs, or to diagnose and identify learning difficulties in students.

All standardized tests are designed to assess students under carefully controlled conditions. This means that all students who write the test will experience the exact same test-writing conditions. In this way, it is assumed that all performance-influencing variables—the time of the day and the year that the test is written, marking procedures, directions stated to the students, test writing tools and materials, and so on—can be controlled, and that the test is a true measure of the students' abilities. Also, before being administered to students, most standardized tests are pre-tested on a sample population and subsequently refined to remove any unclear or problematic questions. By standardizing the testing conditions, it is assumed that test results are likely to be more reliable than the results of teacher-made tests.

Criterion-referenced and Norm-referenced Tests

With criterion-referenced testing, an individual student's test score is compared to standards of proficiency, and the score is not influenced by the performance of other test-takers. Criterion-referenced tests tend to focus on what the student is capable of doing and on mastery of the subject. Educators may also purchase criterion-referenced tests from publishers to evaluate students on units of instruction in their own classrooms; however, the teacher's use of such professionally designed tests does not release the teacher from covering the school district's prescribed curriculum goals. Nor should an individual teacher use a standardized test to evaluate a student's academic proficiency and determine a letter grade when the relevant skills and knowledge have not been taught to the test-taker.

Norm-referenced tests, on the other hand, compare a student's performance to the performance of other students. The purpose of the norm-referenced test is to differentiate between individual students, and this is accomplished by having a

Some commonly recognized standardized academic achievement tests are the Scholastic Aptitude Test (SAT), the Stanford Achievement Test, and the Iowa Test of Basic Skills.

Criterion-referenced tests may be marked using one of several approaches: the number of correct answers, the speed of the performance, the quality of the performance, or the precision and accuracy of the performance.

If all the test questions were easy, and all students could answer most of the questions correctly, then an educator would not be able to rank the performance of the students.

high variability of scores. In order to discriminate between the test-takers, the test questions must usually be quite difficult. However, by asking difficult test questions, the educator may tend to omit test questions that evaluate simple but important content or skills taught in the class. Norm-referenced tests may be used, for example, to determine a student's relative strength or weakness in different subject areas. They may also be used to determine a student's academic growth and progress over a period of several years.

Norm Samples

Before giving a standardized test to students in the general population, it is administered to a large sample of test-takers who are similar to the students who will be writing the test in the schools. This group of sample test writers is called the norm sample, and serves as a comparison group for students who will be taking the actual test. This means that if an actual test-taker in a school receives an "average" score on the test, then his or her score is average compared to what was average for the sample population. Of course, for a norm-referenced score to have any meaning, the reference group must be known.

Using an Old Norm Sample

Digging around in some old boxes in the dusty bowels of the school basement, Principal S found and subsequently encouraged the teachers of his inner-city school to use a standardized reading test that—unbeknownst to him—was ten years old. The front cover of each test booklet had been removed by the former administrator in preparation for discarding. Despite this, Principal S suggested that the teachers could still use these tests to measure student reading proficiency. One teacher even suggested that it might be a good idea to use the students' test results to calculate report-card grades.

Theoretically, a student can belong to any number of reference groups—age, gender, socio-economic, linguistic, and so on—and the subgroups that comprise a norm sample must be known if the test results are to have any meaning.

Fortunately for the principal in this case, several seasoned teaching veterans realized that the test was a decade old and, therefore, would not provide teachers and parents with accurate results. The reason for this was simple: the principal had chosen a test with a norm sample that possibly did not represent the teachers' own groups of test-takers. Some test publishing companies that create and sell standardized tests to school districts use different definitions of what a national norm sample means. In fact, given the diversity of today's classrooms, no publisher's norm sample can truly reflect an "average" classroom. The principal in the above case also failed to recognize that norm samples are time sensitive. This means that, as time passes, social and economic factors may change, thereby changing the conditions—and possibly the achievement—experienced by students. The principal erred in assuming that old norm samples would necessarily give him a reliable standard to which he could evaluate students.

Standardized Test Scores

Everyone talks about the importance of standardized tests, but few people—including teachers—really understand the subject. For the classroom teacher, understanding—and in many cases, justifying—standardized test scores is often a simple matter of self-preservation, since the public tends to see student

Most teachers and parents agree that high test scores are important, but for the most part, few of them seem able to explain what a high test score (or a low test score, for that matter) represents.

success as a reflection of teacher ability. A teacher who possesses a basic knowledge of standardized tests and their associated scoring methods is able to rationalize better the test's use in the classroom, to explain the test's purpose, to evaluate student achievement, to plan remedial instruction, and to defend teaching performance.

The Average

Upon returning any marked test to students, a teacher will usually hear a flurry of inquisitive voices excitedly asking, "What did you get? What did you get?" Almost reflexively, students compare their marks with one another. Success, it would seem, is a relative concept, and somehow a score of 70% is all the more meaningful to a student when other students received scores considerably lower. As adults, most of us can relate: "It is bad enough that I should fail, but worse that my friends should succeed." Likewise, parents and students often interpret test scores against the backdrop of the average score. Yet really, the concept of an average can be deceptive, as it tends not to reveal any meaningful educational information about the individual test-taker.

Teachers must be cautious when they talk about an average simply because the term can have three different meanings:

- The average score might refer to an arithmetic calculation, whereby all the scores are added together and then divided by the total number of test-takers [e.g., $(20 + 20 + 30 + 35 + 50) \div 5 = 31$]. This type of average is referred to as the *mean*.
- The average might represent a mark that is midpoint in a series of marks (e.g., in the series 20, 20 30, 35, 50, the score of 30 is physically in the middle of the list). This is called the *median* and can best be remembered if one thinks of a highway median running between two stretches of road.
- The third type of average, called the *mode*, is simply the score that shows up the most often in a series (for example, in the test scores 10, 20, 20, 40, 50, 50, 50, the mode is 50.)

Teachers must be very careful when discussing class averages with parents and students—they do not give an accurate representation of relative performance.

So, what does all of this mean for teachers? The problem with any form of an average is that no information is provided on how similar the various student scores are to one another. In other words, averages tell the teacher or parent very little about the relative achievement of the test-taker, and fails to account for the influence of very high or very low scores. Also, in order to appreciate what is average for any particular group, one must know the characteristics of that group. Finally, an average can be motivationally counterproductive for both students and teachers as it fails to address the underlying causes of success and failure. An average fails to account for a student's personal growth and development, and the unique circumstances of the individual learner.

The Normal Distribution and the Bell Curve

Norm-referenced evaluation on standardized tests may rely on the bell curve to rank the performance of students. As can be seen in The Normal Curve on page 68, the majority of test scores fall in the middle at the graph's hump. The centre line represents the average, or mean. As one progresses toward the end-points (called the *tails*), one finds fewer and fewer scores. With the bell curve, a teacher knows, in advance of giving the test, the percentage of scores that will fall within each part of the curve.

The normal distribution has led to numerous types of scoring methods for norm-referenced standardized tests. A brief introduction to these scoring methods will help you better understand what these scores truly represent, and will help you not to misinterpret the meaning of norm-referenced student test scores.

Percentile Rank

The percentile rank (PR) probably is the easiest scoring method to explain to parents. The PR indicates the percentage of students in the norm sample that received a score below the raw score obtained by an individual test-taker (see The Normal Curve below). For example, a student who received a PR of 92 did better than 92 percent of the other students; a student with a PR of 50 did better than 50 percent of the norm sample and received an average grade.

THE NORMAL CURVE

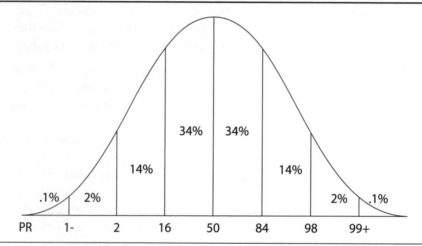

| PR | 1- | 2 | 16 | 50 | 84 | 98 | 99+ |

The centre line at the graph's hump represents the average score. The percentile rank (PR) indicates a student's rank per 100 students starting from the bottom of the distribution. A PR of 50 would indicate an average score.

It is important to recognize that the differences in PR in the middle of the normal distribution curve tend to be over interpreted. One could imagine an individual being required to rank the order of 100 children running in a 100-meter race; it would be easy to rank the order of the fastest and the slowest runners, but it would be very difficult to determine who would place 50th and who would place 51st. Likewise, a PR test score of 50 and one of 60, though they may sound like a large difference in performance, may in fact represent only a difference of one or two points in the students' raw scores.

Similarly, at the upper and lower extremes of performance—the tails of the normal curve—small differences in percentile rank can actually represent large differences in raw scores. (Using the running race analogy once again, a PR of 99 can mean the difference of many minutes compared to a PR of 96.) As a result, teachers frequently misinterpret the PR differences when they occur at the ends of the tails. Finally, percentile ranks are always specific to a particular group; therefore, in order for the score to have any meaningful context, the teacher must be able to define the nature of the group in question.

Z-Scores and Standard Deviations

While percentile ranks are difficult to interpret and can not be used to make accurate comparisons among ranks, a *z-score* compares each individual's raw score in relation to its distance from the mean, or the average score. In other words, a z-score informs the student how far he or she is from the mean score.

A z-score uses positive numbers when the student's raw score is above the average, and negative numbers when it is below the average. A z-score of 0 means it is exactly average (see The Z-Score below). A z-score uses a *standard deviation* that informs the test-taker how spread out around the mean all of the scores are. For example, the student test scores 45, 46, 49, 50, 51, 53, 55 have a smaller standard deviation than a set of test scores with the distribution 10, 45, 49, 80, 82, 90, 92. Clearly, in the first set of scores, the raw scores do not vary greatly from the mean; in the second set of scores, the variation is greater.

THE Z-SCORE

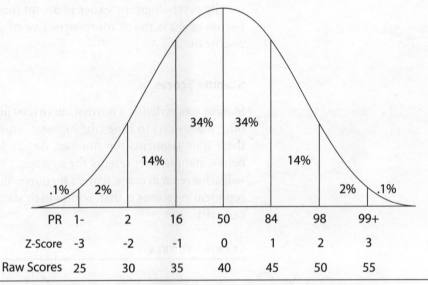

PR	1-	2	16	50	84	98	99+
Z-Score	-3	-2	-1	0	1	2	3
Raw Scores	25	30	35	40	45	50	55

The z-score represents a student's individual score in relation to the group mean.

As can be seen in The Z-Score, a student with a z-score of +1 is at the 84th percentile, and 34% of the scores fall within this category. A student with a z-score of -2 is at the 2nd percentile and is well below the average. Likewise, 14% of students will fall between +1 and +2 standard deviations, and only 2% will fall between +2 and +3 standard deviations. Less than 1% of the individuals will achieve above the +3 standard deviation. It is apparent that 68% of all test-takers will necessarily fall between -1 and +1.

When using z-scores, one standard deviation above the average is written as z = +1.0. This means that the student with a z-score of +1 did very well on the test compared to other students, simply because few students, generally speaking, get higher than +1. However, a score of -1 or lower means that the student did much worse on the test compared to the other test-takers. A set of student scores with a large standard deviation (let us say 20) represents a large spread of scores (i.e., a large variability) around the mean; a small standard deviation (let us say 5) represents a spread of scores that are closer to the mean. In The Z-Score figure above, it is apparent that the mean is 40 and that the standard deviation is 5 (i.e., 45 - 40 = 5). This implies that a student who received a score of 45 is at the +1 standard deviation. A student with a score of 50 is at the +2 standard deviation and is at the 98th percentile.

So, what does this imply for the teacher trying to explain to a concerned parent why Johnny got a z-score of -1?

- As with all scores derived from a normal distribution, one half of the population must score below the mean, regardless of student or teacher ability.

- A score that is dependent on a normal curve tells the teacher little about subject mastery and the student's ability to meet specific criteria.
- The teacher must ensure that the norm sample from which the scores were derived adequately represents the population of test-takers in relation to subgroups and the time frame.
- In order to put the student's score into clearer perspective and to be able to create a plan for the student's academic improvement, the teacher needs to be familiar with the student's unique background and educational history.

T-Scores

Like the z-score, the t-score is a way to standardize scores, but without the inconvenience of using negative numbers. With the t-score, the mean is 50 (instead of 0 as with the z-score) and uses a standard deviation of 10. Therefore, a t-score of 60 would be equivalent to a z-score of +1. In many circumstances, this method of scoring can be much more attractive to all people concerned, as a positive score is usually psychologically easier to accept than a negative number. For example, a t-score of 30 is much more attractive to parents and students compared to a z-score of -2.

Stanine Scores

Stanine scores divide a normal curve into nine segments that are numbered from one (the lowest) to nine (the highest). Student scores can be assigned to one of these nine segments, or *stanines*. As can be seen in the figure Stanine Scores below, stanine 5 represents the average. This means that 20% of the test-takers will achieve an average score. Of course, the obvious concern with this form of representing scores is that, within each stanine, a wide variety of different scores can exist.

STANINE SCORES

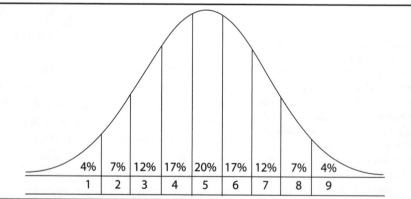

A normal distribution can be divided into nine sections, or stanines. A student's score can be assigned to one of these sections.

Grade-Equivalent Scores

Most parents would readily assume that they had raised a genius if a test administered to their son's or daughter's class revealed that their child was performing four grades above his or her current grade level. Sadly, the reality may be a bit of a let down for some parents and their young scholars. Tests that represent student performance as a grade-equivalent score reflect the average score, or expected ability, for a student in a particular grade.

Grade-equivalent scores are represented as a whole number—which represents the grade level—and a decimal—which represents a month of the school year. A student who obtains a grade equivalent score of 10.8 would be interpreted as performing at the equivalent of a student in the tenth grade and at the eighth month of the school year. Since a grade-equivalent score is obtained from an average of the scores for the norm sample, it is norm-referenced; some students necessarily must be at the fiftieth percentile.

Several concerns regarding grade-equivalent scores need to be addressed:

- This method of scoring can vary from subject to subject. A student may do well in one subject, but poorly in another.
- Students in different grades take different tests that cover different topics and content. This means that a Grade 10 student who obtains a score of 12.1 is not necessarily performing at the twelfth-grade level. In this hypothetical example, the Grade 10 student did not in fact write the same test as did the Grade 12 students. Therefore, the test written by the student in Grade 10 reports nothing about how well he would do on an actual Grade 12 test; it means only that the student has a superior knowledge of Grade 10 concepts.
- The validity of the grade-equivalent score depends greatly on the closeness of fit between the test's contents and the material taught to the students by the teacher during the year and by other teachers in previous years.
- Individual students cognitively mature at different rates, and this maturation rate may be due to biological or environmental factors. Grade-equivalent scores operate under the faulty premise that growth occurs for all students at the same rate over the course of the year.

The Confidence Band

It is likely that most parents would lose all confidence in the education system if they received a report card from their child's teacher stating that their son's or daughter's academic achievement is somewhere between 8 and 88%. Yet, ironically, such reporting would be more honest and accurate than trying to represent student achievement with a single symbolic letter from the alphabet. A *confidence band*, or *confidence interval*, accounts for possible error in a test.

Since no standardized test can be completely error free, it is impossible for an educator to state with certainty a student's true ability. A student who receives a test score of 73% one day, may receive a score of 88% on the same test on a different day due to a host of factors. The confidence band is used to try to address this discrepancy in performance by indicating what the student's true ability might be. The value of a confidence band is perhaps best understood by comparing a student's test results to a thermometer reading on a warm summer day. Different thermometers will indicate slightly different temperatures due to a variety of factors: the structural differences of each thermometer, the location of each thermometer at the time of being read, the directions given to each individual observer, the quality of the eyesight of the individuals reading the thermometers, and so on. The Confidence Band on page 72 shows a two-level confidence band: the thicker band indicates that the student's score probably lies somewhere

Grade-equivalent scores reflect the average score, or expected ability, for a student in a particular grade.

A grade-equivalent score is given to a norm sample perhaps only twice during the year, which means that the scores for the other months of the year must be extrapolated from these results.

A confidence band represents a range of scores that most likely represents a student's achievement on a particular test.

between 19 and 66, while the narrower band gives an even higher probability that the student's true score lies somewhere between 8 and 84.

CONFIDENCE BAND

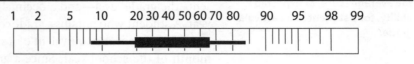

A confidence band shows the probable ability of a student.

Most tests will not report student scores to parents and students using confidence bands simply because they appear vague and give the impression that the test—or worse, the educator—is unable to provide a clear evaluation of the student's ability. However, the confidence band underscores the notion that no single form of evaluation can be error free and be a true representation of a student's ability. For this reason, no single test should be used as the sole measure of a student's comprehension of a course's goals.

TEACHER TIPS

To protect themselves from claims of incompetence and from being turned into scapegoats when, in fact, they have steadfastly and faithfully taught the stated goals of the curriculum guide in a pedagogically sound manner, teachers should consider the specific questions below.

• **Does the test have content validity?** The teacher must be certain that the individual items on the test reflect the course objectives taught to the students. Likewise, a teacher should consider the adequacy of instruction received by the students in previous grades. If previous teachers from previous years failed to impart important skills and concepts, then student performance may suffer.

• **Is it clear what the test measures?** Different tests measure different aspects of student achievement, and simply relying on the test's title to determine content usually is insufficient. For example, though several English tests may all purport to measure reading comprehension, one test may emphasize critical thinking skills, while another might stress decoding skills. No two tests measure exactly the same thing, and the only way to fully appreciate what any test measures is to review the test item by item. Therefore, it stands to reason that scores obtained on two different tests should be compared to one another only with caution, as they likely represent different aspects of ability.

• **Is the norm sample appropriate and representative of the test-takers?** The definition of the test publisher's norm sample must be stated clearly, for the closer the fit between the sample population and the test-takers, the more confidently may a teacher interpret the results. Teachers should keep in mind that many standardized tests are created for the purpose of making the publisher money; therefore, it is to the publisher's benefit to cast the net as widely as possible when creating norm samples. The danger, of course, is that many norm samples —such as a "national" norm sample—are too general and do not adequately represent the vast array of subgroups that exist.

• **Was the correct norm table used?** Many tests provide norm tables that allow the teacher to convert a student's raw score into a norm-referenced score. At times, teachers have made the mistake of using the wrong table or simply misreading it.

• **Were proper standardized testing procedures followed?** Even small deviations in the management of the test setting can influence student scores. Individual teachers must be careful not to express to students their own dismissive, critical thoughts regarding the test in the weeks or days leading up to the exam setting, as this can deflate student motivation.

• **Are the terms used to describe student achievement clearly defined?** Many criterion-reference tests use terms such as *Fully Meets Expectations* and *Not Yet Meets Expectations*. The teacher should be able to explain the meaning of these labels.

• **Are the unique characteristics of the individual student recognized?** To fully understand why a student received a particular score, the teacher should be familiar with the student's personal background and educational deficiencies. A child's low test score might be explained by a problem in his or her home life, for instance. If the teacher suspects that the child is experiencing stress or academic setbacks due to personal circumstances, then these suspicions should be documented in writing. Likewise, the teacher must take into account the timing of the test in relation to other events occurring in the student's life; students who write a test at the beginning of a two-week long exam period might fare better than students, suffering from fatigue, who write the same test at the end of the exam schedule.

• **Is the group of students academically low functioning?** Simply put, some classes are academically capable and some are not. At some point in his or her career, every teacher, for whatever reason, will have the proverbial class from hell—students who are more interested in drawing graffiti on their desks than drawing conclusions from their assigned reading. When a teacher has a large number of students who are under-achievers, then the classroom mean will likely be affected.

• **How does the individual student's test score compare to his or her performance in the classroom?** A more thorough and complete interpretation of a student's test score and abilities can be determined when viewed against the backdrop of classroom performance during and across the years.

• **Is it clear why students are being evaluated with this particular standardized test?** The teacher needs to be able to rationalize the use of the test, state its purpose, and have a clear vision of what ultimately will be done with the test's results.

Teaching to the Test

A Surprising Improvement

Standardized test results for students from an inner-city elementary school showed a remarkable 63% improvement in student math scores, and a 45% improvement in reading ability, when compared to test results from the previous year. District administrators found these increases perplexing, as the conditions of the population had not changed. Upon closer inspection, it became evident to investigators that classroom teachers had been given access to the test in the weeks leading up to the official examination date, and had used their knowledge of the exam content to impart specific exam questions to the students. Furthermore, it became apparent that the principal, feeling pressure from his superiors to raise test scores, had encouraged teachers to "teach to the test."

"Teaching to the test," as shown in A Surprising Improvement, is clearly problematic, since it is not student achievement that is being measured. However, feeling pressure from parents and administrators to achieve higher test scores, many teachers will tailor instruction to fit the parameters of a specific examination. "Teaching to the test" by this second definition is acceptable, and may even

Teachers and parents often mistakenly assume that a standardized test is the Holy Grail of academic achievement and represents some absolute, definitive benchmark to which all students should aspire and be measured against.

characterize effective teaching. Clearly, the teacher must try and strike some sort of balance between the course goals and the standardized test.

Practising with Previous Tests

The American satirist Mark Twain famously observed that there are three kinds of lies in this world: "Lies, damn lies, and statistics." Statistics, like any method for reporting data, are prone to errors of methodology and observation. Take the IQ test, for instance; common wisdom tells us that intelligence is a stable trait and can not be enhanced through training and studying, yet people can increase their IQ scores when they receive coaching in their test-writing and problem-solving skills. So, too, can students increase their standardized test scores by increasing their familiarity with the test's format, procedures, and requirements.

Student performance on standardized tests increases when the following conditions are met by the teacher:

- the students are adequately prepared for the test in both knowledge and procedure
- students are told what content and skills will be assessed
- students are told the reason for the assessment
- students are told how the results will be used
- students are provided the opportunity to practise writing previous examinations or examinations that have similar content and require similar skills

Evaluation Complaints

Given the high value that parents and students place on school marks, the evaluation of student work at times is less an issue of pedagogy than of politics—and, as the saying goes, politics makes for strange bedfellows. Borrowing a business analogy, the modern-day school administrator tends to see schools as providing a service to their valued consumers (i.e., parents and students), and often great effort is made to make the customer feel contented. The teacher operates in a political arena and so must, at times, make astute political maneuvers and decisions. The teacher must keep a finger on the pulse of the school community, remain vigilant regarding parental concerns, and address them decisively when they first arise. Teachers must ensure that seemingly minor complaints are addressed in a timely manner, and that they do not transmogrify into larger issues of teacher competency and integrity.

When it comes to passing judgment on the academic abilities of other people's children, sometimes discretion is the better part of diplomacy. Stubbornly locking horns with a parent over a child's mark can be counterproductive, as it may distract one from the job of teaching, polarize members of the school community, and even leave in tatters one's own reputation. Of course, this does not mean that teachers should kowtow to the marking demands of parents.

Providing that the teacher is following established, accepted evaluation and teaching practices in the classroom, then that teacher, in theory at least, has great autonomy in deciding the marks that he or she issues. However, in the interest of public relations and in an effort to appease parental concerns, the teacher or principal might consider subjecting the student's work to a structured, formal re-marking process.

Even at universities, where the courses are taught by experts with doctoral degrees, the potential for marking error is recognized and a clear protocol exists for resolving student complaints. When a dispute arises regarding the mark awarded to a specific assignment, the teacher or principal might consider following these steps:

1. The complainant contacts the teacher who did the marking. If a parent or student has a concern about the teacher's marking, then protocol usually dictates that the complainant first discusses the issue with the teacher who did the marking. If the principal is first approached, then the principal should redirect the complainant to the teacher. This sends the clear message that the teacher is competent and in control of the situation. Only if the matter cannot be resolved during a private meeting with the teacher should the principal become involved.

2. A second, qualified marker is found. At the high-school level, the duty of finding a second marker often rests with the department head. The identity of this marker often is kept confidential.

3. The complainant is informed of the process and possible consequences. Some schools state that a student must accept the second marker's grade, even if it is lower than the original mark. This is done to prevent students and parents from abusing the re-marking process.

4. The complainant submits a letter of contention. This letter should detail the complainant's request and his reasons for the request.

5. The complainant submits a copy of the assignment to be re-marked. Ideally, this copy should be an unblemished, "clean" copy of the original work, so as not to prejudice the second marker. The complainant should submit the work in question to the department head or to some neutral teacher.

6. The second marker receives a copy of the original instructions given to the students and the marking criteria. The work is then evaluated.

7. The complainant and the subject teacher are informed of the second marker's evaluation. The Confidential Re-evaluation Report on page 92 should be completed by the second marker when a student's work is evaluated for a second time. To ensure accuracy, transparency, and accountability in the re-marking process, this second marker, before returning the newly marked work, should make sure that each task has been completed and checked off.

The School Power Structure

In the public relations game of teaching, things can go from bad to worse in unpredictable ways. Small, seemingly insignificant problems and complaints can quickly spread and mutate along unforeseen tangents, soon threatening to engulf the teacher, if not the entire school community. This potential for volatility in the school setting is one reason why school principals tend to define a good teacher not necessarily as someone who teaches well, but as someone who is socially adroit with parents, students, and other teachers. Principals, teachers, and school board members must listen to, respect, and often act on the opinions, concerns, and complaints of the community. Of course, at times, this can place the principal or school administrator in an awkward situation, having to walk a line between recognized educational practice and the demands of parents.

The Request for Re-evaluation of Student Work on page 91 should be completed by a student or parent prior to a formal re-evaluation. This form should accompany the work to be re-evaluated and be given to the second marker.

More than at any other time in the past, the education system has become a hotbed of competing interests, and never before have students, their parents, and special interest groups possessed such powerful voices in regard to influencing schools and educational policy.

Parents and the public vote for members of the school board

↓

School Board

School board members are elected by the public. The school board represents the views and concerns of the voters. Board members set and implement educational policies.

↓

Superintendent (Director of Schools)

The school board members hire the school superintendent or influence the current superintendent. The superintendent is responsible for managing and directing the entire school district. The superintendent can be fired by the school board.

↓

Principals

The superintendent is responsible for hiring and firing school principals and vice-principals. A principal has the following duties: maintaining school order and discipline, supervising teachers and vice-principals, maintaining the health and safety of the students and staff, promoting community relations, record-keeping, holding examinations, writing school budgets.

↓

Department Heads

The principal selects department heads from interested, qualified teachers. Principals and department heads make sure that individual teachers are teaching the course goals and are using proper educational practices.

↓

Teachers

Teachers teach their students the goals of the curriculum guide. Teachers develop their own *specific goals* and lesson plans in order to teach the course. Teachers are responsible for classroom management.

As can be seen from The Political Power Structure of the Public School System, administrators in the education power structure must toe the current educational line of the day and ensure that the educational practices of the school are in harmony with the demands and expectations of the community and society. Principals must be careful to listen to the opinions and complaints of parents, at times as a polite exercise in diplomacy, and at other times out of genuine concern. However, principals always want parents to feel as though their concerns are being addressed. It is to the principal's advantage for all interested stakeholders—parents, students, and teachers—to believe that they are contributing members of the school community and that their concerns and issues are taken seriously. For the principal to do his or her job, the perception of social harmony must prevail.

Mobs, Scapegoats, and Principals

Occupying the lowest rung of the school power structure, teachers must take precautions to ensure that they are not made the proverbial sacrificial lamb in the administration's attempt to placate a parent's concerns. Other members of the school community easily may be co-opted, often unwittingly, into the complaint process. This seems to be especially true in elementary schools where inexperienced, hyper-vigilant parents operating in closed, tight-knit social networks may be influenced by, and reflect, one another's nascent but evolving concerns and anxieties.

A Mass Parental Movement

In a small, socially tight-knit community, an experienced teacher with a spotless professional record had a complaint filed against him by the parent of one of his students. This parent believed that the teacher had unfairly given her daughter low marks on several assignments. The principal investigated the matter and concluded that the teacher's marking was fair and accurate. Shortly after this informal investigation, the principal wrote a note of encouragement to the teacher in which she stated: "I greatly enjoyed your lessons. You are doing a lot of good in this community. It is important for you to convey this good work to parents. Well done." However, over the next three months, some 42 complaints—ranging from bias in marking to poor lesson planning—were filed by numerous parents regarding this same teacher. The principal, who only a few months earlier had praised the work of the teacher, requested that the teacher transfer to a new school, citing her concerns regarding the teacher's competency. These concerns were stated in a letter she wrote to the teacher: "The lack of showcasing student work; poor lunch hour behavior of students; cleanliness of the classroom; distribution of oral questions between boys and girls in the classroom; the amount of time the teacher is out of the classroom during instructional time; prompt dissemination of information home." Interestingly, 41 of the 42 complainants did not have, nor ever did have, a child in this teacher's class.

Only too often has a teacher in good faith sat down with parents and a principal in an effort to rationally explain how a child's mark was derived only to find himself waylaid and assailed by a barrage of unforeseen and unwarranted abuses and accusations.

The principal in this case chose the path of political expedience and dismissed the teacher, not for reasons of professional misconduct, but to satisfy community demands. Clearly, the role of the principal in mediating and resolving parent/teacher conflicts is often paramount to a peaceful resolution for all. The problem for the teacher arises, however, when the school administrator allows personal loyalties and popular sentiment to sway his or her decisions.

When a school administrator, whether formally or informally, investigates a teacher's instructional and evaluation practices, the teacher in question must ensure that transparency, accuracy, and honesty prevail throughout the investigative process. If any meeting should be held by a school administrator regarding a teacher's performance, it is incumbent upon the teacher to be proactive, and to take the necessary precautions to ensure an atmosphere of integrity.

TEACHER TIPS

Before participating in any meeting with a principal and parents regarding the teacher's classroom procedures, the teacher in question should consider the following recommendations:

• **The teacher should learn about the school district's established procedures for resolving parental complaints and the investigation of teachers.** School administrators must follow the procedures as outlined in school board policy, acts of legislation, or a written contract.

When meeting with parents and students regarding a teacher's performance, the teacher and administrator may wish to complete the Teacher/Parent Meeting Agenda form on page 90. Section B of the form should be completed prior to the meeting.

While most teachers would probably prefer to play the role of the "good guy" and be the bearer of only good news, the teacher, to do his or her job responsibly, should report to parents the student's true abilities and shortcomings. Failure to do so would render grades and evaluation hollow and meaningless.

• **The teacher must ensure that the school administrator has informed him or her of any and all complaints and accusations.** The teacher should receive and keep copies of any letters or memos that directly or indirectly address the teacher's performance.

• **If a teacher is to attend a meeting with an administrator and a parent, then the meeting's agenda must be stated and followed.** By following the stated agenda, a resolution usually can be reached quickly, and the threat of "teacher bashing" avoided.

• **It must be clear whether the teacher or the principal will chair the meeting.** In order to remain true to the stated agenda, control of the meeting must be kept in the hands of a school employee.

• **The teacher should avoid meeting with a group of complainants.** If several families or students wish to meet with the teacher, then separate meetings should be arranged. A teacher who meets with a large group of complainants runs the risk of galvanizing feelings of social cohesion among the complainants and fostering possible group hostility.

• **The teacher should extricate himself or herself from the meeting should the complainants become verbally hostile or refuse to respect the meeting's agenda.** All workers have the legal right to a workplace setting that is safe and respectful.

• **The teacher should refrain from discussing the performance of another student.** Some complainants will wish to compare the marks of various students to show marking bias or inconsistency. The teacher should cite issues of student confidentiality and simply refer to the stated marking criteria as justification.

• **The teacher needs to recognize the right to have representation.** In meetings that are expected to be especially onerous, the teacher may wish to have a fellow teacher, a union representative, or legal counsel present and taking notes. This has the advantage of providing a gentle show of force, while also providing a witness should things go awry.

• **The teacher should keep all written memos, letters, and records that relate to the teacher or the meeting.** In the case A Mass Parental Movement on page 78, the teacher, by producing previously written notes and memos, was able to throw into question the principal's true intent.

• **The teacher must never become hostile or emotional during the meeting.** A calm, professional demeanor must be maintained even in the face of growing parental hostility or obstinacy. The teacher must appear reasonable and be careful not to give the meeting's participants any reason for concern or recrimination.

Operationalizing Evaluation Complaints

Some parents attempt to rationalize their child's low grade by throwing into question the teacher's ability or even integrity. "Not my child!" seems at times to be an almost instinctive protective response of some parents. The child is a natural extension of the parent, and any evaluation of the child that does not reflect the parent's favorable vision may be perceived by that parent as a direct attack on his or her child-rearing practices, or even personal identity. Some parents also correctly interpret a low mark as potentially narrowing the child's future education or career choices.

Whether teachers like to admit it or not, the teacher most often is perceived by individuals living within the boundaries of the school community as an outsider, both geographically and socially. Teachers are often transient as they move from school to school throughout their careers, failing to develop deep meaningful roots and a shared common history with the adult members of the community. Even those teachers who have lived in the school area for decades may be socially disconnected from the community, due to the perceived authority that they have over the community's children; consequently, they may be disfranchised from the perks associated with group membership. This social disconnection is especially true with the divergent social worlds of the teacher and his students. While teacher and students may be in contact with one another in the same room for five or six hours a day, students have their own subculture and their own loyalties that differ markedly from those of the teacher.

Every teacher in his or her career must contend with the occasional isolated complaint; however, the real potential for harm occurs when a trickle turns in to a deluge.

Parental Retaliation

Over the course of the academic year, a public school teacher grew increasingly hesitant to give one of his students—a popular boy named Tam—a mark below 70% on any of his submitted assignments for fear of parental retaliation. The only times this teacher heard from Tam's parents were on those occasions when he issued a "low mark" to any of Tam's work. While the marks awarded to Tam accurately reflected his academic performance, on each occasion that a "low mark" was issued by the teacher, Tam's parents would launch a well-orchestrated campaign designed to damage the teacher's professional reputation and to throw into question the adequacy of instruction. The parents' tactics included numerous meetings with the principal and the teacher, letters to the superintendent of schools, and a "whisper campaign" among the community's parents. Towards the end of the year, Tam was frequently observed actively trying to recruit classmates to his cause, and on numerous occasions he would personally escort small groups of students down to the school's office so that they could share with the principal their tales of the teacher's supposed evaluation abuses.

How can a teacher defend evaluation decisions when faced with multiple complaints that stem from group loyalty and simple opportunism? Too often, it would seem, administrators fall back on the quaint, but not too reliable, adage that where there is smoke there is fire; if numerous students or parents file complaints about a teacher, then there must be some truth behind the accusations, they reason. In a court of law, an accused person is not required to prove his or her innocence; it is, of course, the job of the prosecutor to present clear, unambiguous evidence of the individual's guilt. Similarly, when a teacher reports on a student's disruptive behavior, good practice dictates that the teacher offers specific, operationalized examples of the offending behavior. This basic tenet must also apply to teachers in the workplace. It is insufficient, if not reckless and provocative, for an administrator to investigate the complaint, for example, that the teacher is an "unfair marker" or that the teacher is biased in favor of other students. These are merely generalized beliefs to which a teacher can not respond convincingly. If a teacher is accused of improperly evaluating student work or dereliction of duty, then that teacher must be informed of the specifics of the accusation: What specific behavior is deemed problematic? When did it occur? Where did it occur? Who were the witnesses?

A student's own words may be used to aid a beleaguered teacher whose evaluation strategies are questioned. Consider the tactic of a teacher when confronted by a slick, fast-talking student who tries to throw into question the accuracy of the teacher's record keeping.

Documenting the Student's Words

One month after the class had written a math test, a student named Samuel, who was absent on the day of the initial test, was informed by the teacher that he still had to write a make-up test. Samuel protested and claimed that he had in fact already written the test, and that the teacher must have lost it or misplaced it. Samuel insisted that he received a score of 84% on the exam. The teacher, knowing full well that Samuel was lying, asked him to write down the details of his complaint on a piece of paper and to sign and date it. In his written summation, Samuel attested to the presence of two other students in his math class—Karen and Susan—who, he claimed, also had missed the original test date and had written the test with him after school. The teacher then compared Samuel's written statement with the office attendance records, and was able to show that Samuel's two alleged co-writers were in fact present during the initial in-class test setting. Samuel, it was proved, was lying.

Maintaining Trust

Which of the two teachers below is the more competent teacher?

Teacher A, who is known for spending more time coaching on the football field than teaching in the classroom, spends fifteen minutes of every class hour in the staff room, socializing and gossiping. Even though he is the department head, he is unaware of course goals and his lessons are poorly developed and delivered. Not surprisingly, his students consistently receive the lowest marks on year-end examinations in comparison with the students of other teachers. Yet he remains popular with students and parents due to his convivial attitude, and because the football team has had a string of wins.

Teacher B has an advanced degree in education and is well-versed in teaching methods and practice. His course is well-organized, and his unit and lesson plans are thoughtfully developed. Concepts are presented to students using a wide variety of instructional techniques, and students are evaluated using clearly established marking criteria and procedures. His students are required to work hard during class time and consistently outperform the students of other teachers.

Most teachers would probably unhesitatingly give thumbs up to Teacher B, since he exhibits those traits of good teaching that all teachers learn during their college years. Unfortunately, credit is not always given where credit is due. While we all like to think of ourselves as rational, thoughtful, and independent thinkers who fairly weigh all the evidence before reaching a conclusion, the standards of evidence that we do accept and rely on to evaluate and respond to our world are most often frightfully weak. It may not be fair, but the "truth" is often a matter of consensus; indeed, the truth frequently tends to be a social construct mediated along lines of interpersonal communication.

When a student, a parent, or even another teacher asserts that Teacher X or Y is an excellent teacher, the listener should try asking how the speaker knows. What evidence allows the speaker to make this assertion? Has the speaker ever observed one of the teacher's lessons? Has the speaker ever seen the test results of the teacher's students? Does the speaker even know what constitutes good teaching? The answers given to these questions are usually quite surprising and revealing. By all empirical measures of achievement, an individual may truly be a gifted teacher, but if in the collective mind of popular sentiment that teacher is deemed incompetent, then his or her every action and evaluative decision will be viewed with suspicion and caution.

The Characteristics of the Effective Teacher

So, what do the characteristics of the effective teacher have to do with evaluation? Everything! Good teaching and good evaluation go hand in hand, and are inseparable from one another. Evaluation informs the teacher of needed instruction, while sound instruction allows for the meaningful evaluation of students. Effective teaching involves more than simply following the steps of a lesson plan. Good teaching—and by implication, evaluation—involves creating connections with parents and students, and understanding their needs on a personal level.

Throughout this book, the argument has been made that the evaluation of student work can not be divorced from the politics of schooling. Evaluation does not just happen and nor is it simply purely objective and free from the taint of perception. Evaluation always occurs within a wider socio-historical arena, often involving complex social relationships that may not be readily apparent to the casual observer. Indeed, the evaluation of students always proceeds much more smoothly and effortlessly when positive relations exist among teachers, parents, and students. A teacher who cultivates feelings of trust among community members inadvertently promotes the community's faith in his or her marking procedures and educational decisions.

The saying "No one notices a clean countertop, only a dirty one" would seem to have implications for the profession of teaching. A teacher can be a master at the craft of teaching, but it takes only one mishandled event—or the perception that an event was mishandled—for the public and school administrators to lose all confidence in that teacher's professional competency and to reinterpret events to fit their newly formed mental schemata. Perception is a slippery slope, as people tend to look for evidence that confirms their suspicions as opposed to that which discounts them. When the public perceives that a teacher is capable and trustworthy, then parents and administrators usually will not feel the need to call into question the teacher's instructional practices. In short, perception has a tendency to become the reality.

> **A teacher's ability to convey his or her own high professional standards, abilities, and expectations is one of the best ways to prevent parents, students, and administrators from feeling the need to question the educational decisions of the teacher.**
>
> **Teachers may feel safe when they shield themselves behind quantified student behaviors—and indeed, must often do so for their own professional protection; however, effective teaching is also an interpersonal endeavor.**

The Community and Perception

The school principal informed Mrs. P, a Grade 5 teacher working in a middle-class neighborhood, that a parent had expressed concerns regarding the learning environment of her classroom. Specifically, the parent believed that Mrs. P had a propensity for embarrassing students in class by calling on them by name to answer her teacher-directed questions. Several days after the principal had informed Mrs. P of the parent's concerns, the principal walked into the teacher's classroom unannounced, sat in an empty desk at the back of the classroom, and took copious amounts of notes as Mrs. P taught a lesson. Later that day, during recess break, the students of Mrs. P's classroom, who had observed the principal's conspicuous presence during the lesson, discussed the incident with much speculation and began to stitch together a possible explanation as to why the principal was observing their teacher. Within the next four weeks, several other parents had expressed to the principal their grave concerns regarding the climate of Mrs. P's classroom.

A subsequent investigation by a school district administrator led to the conclusion that Mrs. P—whom he described as a capable and thoughtful teacher—and the community members had been unwitting victims of a faulty perceptual feedback loop characterized by circular reasoning. In other words, the principal's presence in Mrs. P's classroom planted the belief in the minds of the community's children and parents that something was amiss, and that this belief, in turn, reinforced and gave credence to the initial parental complaint. (After all, the principal would not be observing Mrs. P unless there were something wrong, the parents reasoned.) It would seem that the initial complaint began to take on a life of its own and threatened to "snowball" uncontrollably into a broader issue of teacher competency.

Teachers must be cognizant of all components of their professional behavior, for when the seed of doubt or suspicion is planted in the public's mind, all aspects of the teacher's performance may be thrown into question. While all teachers learn the same educational theories and, for the most part, use the same educational techniques, some teachers, due to their personality traits, backgrounds, and organizational abilities, are better at teaching and evaluating students, and at gaining the confidence of parents, than are others. Of course, the effective teacher also is one who produces students who are academically capable. While many of the characteristics that contribute to effective teaching are difficult to define and at times can not be readily learned in a teacher-training program, the following twenty characteristics have been shown to promote and enhance teacher effectiveness and parental satisfaction:

1. The teacher has advanced content knowledge in the subject area. In math, science, and English, teachers with advanced knowledge turn out students who perform better on standardized tests. Teachers who are knowledgeable in their subject area are better prepared to answer student questions and can better explain concepts. It is also thought that these teachers become less nervous and are less vague in their explanations, and these characteristics have been shown to influence student performance.

2. The teacher possesses at least three years of teaching experience. A more experienced teacher is not necessarily better than a less experienced teacher. However, generally speaking, teachers with fewer than three to five years of teaching experience are less effective than teachers with more than three to five years of experience. Experienced teachers tend to know better what teaching practices and activities to use when teaching particular concepts. They are also better able to individualize instruction to meet the needs of each student.

3. The teacher displays articulate speech. Teachers with high verbal ability and who have a large vocabulary tend to produce students who perform better on standardized tests.

4. The teacher displays enthusiasm. Teachers who display enthusiasm for both teaching and for their subject area motivate students to study. Enthusiasm may be characterized by rapid and excited vocal delivery, use of hand gestures, varied eye contact, and a high energy level. Teacher enthusiasm also leads to increased memory retention among students.

5. The teacher has a caring attitude. Perhaps the most basic characteristic of the effective teacher is the conspicuous display of a genuinely caring attitude. The effective teacher is truly interested in the well-being and personal lives of students. The caring educator listens to the concerns of students and parents, and displays gentleness. A warm classroom environment is apparent and students may be involved in decision-making for some activities. The caring teacher will most often attend extra-curricular activities, such as concerts and sport events.

6. The teacher displays a sense of fun and play. The joy the teacher receives from the job is evident from a good-natured personality. The teacher participates in activities with students, has a good sense of humor, and will often laugh with students.

7. The teacher works collaboratively with other teachers and parents. A teacher who works with other professionals is able to share educational ideas and has a better awareness of available teaching resources. Likewise, the effective teacher will accept constructive suggestions from colleagues and parents. The effective teacher acknowledges any mistakes he or she may make and corrects them immediately.

8. The teacher displays a desire to further his or her own education or to improve teaching skills. The effective teacher models enthusiasm for learning by attending educational conferences, and willingly receives in-service training to remain up-to-date in the education field. The teacher sees learning as an ongoing process that applies not only to students, but also to teachers.

9. The teacher has a classroom that is structurally well organized to maximize teaching time. Commonly used resources and materials—such as dictionaries, paper, scissors, and so on—are placed in highly accessible areas in order to minimize classroom disruption. Student desks are arranged in a way that maximizes teaching effectiveness.

10. The teacher posts rules in the classroom. The effective teacher will most often spend part of the first week of class informing students of the rules and procedures of the class. In this way, students know what is expected from them and the teacher does not need to waste time later in the year discussing routine, daily procedures.

11. The teacher posts student work on the classroom walls. In order to enhance student motivation and to help students feel as though they are part of the learning process, the effective teacher displays the work of all the students. The teacher routinely changes display work in order to reflect the students' recent learning.

12. The teacher keeps transition time between activities to a minimum. In order not to waste instructional time, the effective teacher ensures a smooth transition between activities with a minimum of disruption. When instructions are clearly articulated, routines are clearly established, and the students understand what is expected of them, the teacher can ensure that a change in activity does not take time away from student learning. Asking students to perform multiple tasks during a one-hour lesson—for example, taking out their homework, marking it as a class, turning it in, and opening their textbooks to a specific page number—can cause a significant loss of instructional time if these tasks are not performed efficiently.

13. The teacher comes to class prepared. The effective teacher is fully prepared to teach on a daily basis. This means that all photocopying and marking is finished before the instructional day begins, and extra materials are available should unforeseen events occur. Any materials needed for a lesson are prepared and organized before instruction.

14. The teacher uses positive reinforcement. While constructive criticism has its place, effective teachers emphasize students' positive qualities, rather than their negative qualities. Students are praised when they perform well and produce work that meets the teacher's expectations.

15. The teacher monitors and controls minor classroom disturbances. The effective teacher is constantly monitoring the behavior of students. Potentially disruptive student behavior is dealt with immediately and prevented from growing into a larger, more serious problem.

16. The teacher circulates throughout the entire classroom. The effective teacher does not sit behind a desk when students are doing seatwork, but takes the initiative and approaches students who may require assistance. The teacher assists students with their work and tries not to spend a disproportionate amount of time with any one student or in any one location of the classroom.

17. The teacher disciplines students fairly and equitably. The effective teacher avoids ridiculing and humiliating students as a method of correction. Rules are applied consistently to all students. Indeed, individuals, and not whole groups, are held accountable for their actions. The rationale behind the rules and penalties are explained to students logically and coherently.

18. The teacher conveys high academic expectations for all students. A student's belief that he or she can succeed is related to personal success. A strong positive correlation exists between a teacher's level of expectation for success and a student's academic achievement. It is not surprising that students in the lowest-achieving 20% of a typical class tend to receive the least amount of attention and encouragement from the teacher. Clearly, the teacher's attitude can create a self-fulfilling prophecy for the student whereby the perceptions and expectations of others influence failure and success.

19. The teacher displays a high level of planning and organization. The teacher is able to inform students and parents what material will be covered in future lessons. Instructional lesson plans are detailed and followed. At the high-school level, especially, a syllabus, or course outline, is given to students at the beginning of the year, and the teacher adheres to it. Also, the teacher's concern for organization and planning is evident in the physical layout of the classroom: the classroom is tidy in appearance, the teacher's desktop is neat and organized, bookshelves are organized, and students are required to keep their desks and notebooks neat and organized.

20. The teacher bases instruction on sound educational theory and practice.
Everything the effective teacher does in the classroom can be defended and justified using research-driven data and findings. A teacher who does not follow recognized educational practice in classroom teaching is doing a disservice to the students and possibly is putting his or her job at risk.

CHECKLIST OF WARNING SIGNS OF AN INEFFECTIVE TEACHER

Warning Signs

Teacher

- Arrives late to school
- Ridicules students
- Is confrontational with students and parents
- Has classroom discipline problems
- Does not display classroom rules or expectations
- Emphasizes rules and consequences only for negative behaviors
- Is unavailable for help outside of school hours
- Spends class time marking papers
- Has a messy classroom
- Does not start teaching at the bell
- Leaves classroom during class time to get supplies
- Has students who appear bored or uninterested
- Applies consequences inconsistently
- Does not display student work or posters on classroom walls
- Does not speak clearly or does not use proper English
- Uses rude or crude speech
- Does not work collaboratively with fellow teachers
- Uses outdated words or materials
- Does not participate in professional growth workshops
- Fails to follow required marking procedures as outlined in this book

The public's perception of the teacher may be influenced by these factors.

The Characteristics of the Effective Student

Success begets success. It is a fact of schooling, but too often it would seem the apple does not fall far from the tree. Just as the cycle of poverty tends to predestine the next generation of children to experience an economic fate similar to their parents, so also do the academically impoverished often come from homes where education is of secondary concern. This is not to say that the parents of underachieving students do not value education in the lives of their children—after all, everyone wants the best for their children—but that they themselves are unable to model the skills and values necessary for academic success and are unsure how to promote learning. However, interventionist, remedial academic programs for at-risk students have clearly shown that students who might otherwise do poorly in school can succeed in their studies. So one must ask the question: Is the great student made or born? Is it nature, or is it nurture? Well, it is probably a mixture of both. Students are not born with the requisite skills, knowledge, and experiences necessary to allow them to recognize and reach their potential; a student must learn how to become successful. Unfortunately, most students fail to recognize their own academic shortcomings and mistakenly believe that they possess adequate to superior study skills, when they do not.

Parents often assume that the education of their child is the sole responsibility of the public-school teacher. They may fail to recognize that a teacher comes in contact with their child only five or six hours out of 24 (and not on all days of the week, at that) for less than one year of the child's life, and certainly not during the developmentally critical first five years of growth. Parents often believe that a teacher knows, or should know, how best to increase the student's achievement, and is able to provide a much-needed magical panacea for academic success. Again, whether it is fair or not, the expectations of parents would seem to have clear implications for the teacher: a teacher should be familiar with *how* students learn to learn, and it is the well-rounded, professionally competent teacher who is well-versed in the metacognitive components of learning. Indeed, some parents are less concerned with whether their child has a grade of A or C- than with how best to improve their child's learning. It is one thing for a teacher to know where the class is heading in terms of content and objectives; it is something else to be able to tell a parent or an administrator the steps the child must take to reach the desired goal. Really, it is an issue of maintaining parental confidence.

What study skills do teachers and educational researchers believe a student should possess in order to improve and excel academically? Students with superior grade point averages tend to exhibit the following ten characteristics:

1. The superior student activates and uses relevant background information and knowledge. Learning new ideas does not take place in a vacuum. Rather, learning proceeds best when new ideas are laid on top of previous learning. Superior students try to see and articulate how the new lesson concept is connected to former ideas discussed in class, to see how classroom learning and ideas are connected to their own lives, and how they might possibly influence the lives of others. Learning is enhanced when the student is able to make a personal, emotional connection to the classroom material.

2. The superior student understands the purpose of reading and studying a specific text. The superior student does not read a text aimlessly, but rather begins the task with a clear goal in mind. When students know what to look for and why, the course readings have a clear context, and relevant information is more likely to become evident.

3. The superior student systematically organizes information and can see some differences between similar ideas. Students can be overwhelmed by the vast array of information that they receive in a course. The ability to categorize data and text information allows students to recall information more quickly and efficiently. By subsuming information under relevant categories, information is chunked and comprehension and memory are enhanced. Also, by organizing the information found in texts and class notes, the student is better able to make connections among various ideas and concepts. Students with high grade point averages often will use the subheadings in their textbooks to help them organize information obtained from classroom lessons and activities.

4. The superior student is able to ignore trivia while focussing on the bigger, more important ideas and themes. By categorizing information, students are able to understand the main ideas behind the details. This is not to say that these students ignore details, such as dates in a history course, or formulae in a math class; rather, they understand the concepts behind the details and how the details relate to the larger ideas and categories. In this way, these students are able to develop and study at the higher cognitive levels of thought (analysis, synthesis, and evaluation).

5. The superior student reads classroom texts and materials critically and looks for internal inconsistencies. In other words, the student is critical of what he or she reads and does not readily accept everything that is read. This is not to say that the student is argumentative and defiant; rather, the superior student weighs the information against prior knowledge and experiences. Superior students read the material critically and skeptically, writing down critical notes in the margins of the text when they question the accuracy, relevance, or perspective of the material or its author.

6. The superior student balances specific details with general information. While the superior student pays particular attention to the theory behind the details, he or she does not ignore the details. Indeed, understanding the details can help the student to better understand the theory or category that is used to organize them. The superior student is able to see how the details, facts, or seemingly trivial bits of information fit into the larger organizing structure. Details and facts are used to provide texture and color to analysis and understanding of the material. By mediating between general theory and details, the superior student is able to detect internal inconsistencies that may exist.

7. Students with superior grade point averages translate new information into images. Imagery is used in the memorization technique of *mnemonics*. With this technique, the student can commit large amounts of detailed information to memory simply by associating objects, events, or people with common items and then putting those items into some sort of visual list. Entire lists of words or events can be memorized by visually associating each word in the list with a particular object and then imagining oneself walking through a room sequentially encountering each object. When it comes time to write the test, the student needs only to visualize walking through the room encountering the various objects in order to recall the required facts and details.

8. Students with superior grades draw and test inferences of many kinds. These students do not immediately assume that they have reached a final, correct conclusion until they have tested several other possible conclusions. They do not assume that their first answer is necessarily the correct one or the only one. They read and review the text and classroom material more than once in order to make new connections with the material and possibly to reach new and different inferences.

9. Superior students are able to self-monitor, evaluate, and improve their learning styles and learning strategies. They recognize when a studying technique works and when it does not. They can consciously select learning styles and strategies to meet the demands of a specific educational task. When they do poorly on an assignment, they are able to self-correct their studying technique to meet the challenges posed by similar assignments in the future. These students are aware of their academic strengths and weaknesses and know how best to improve them. When they do not know how to improve their strategies in order to complete successfully a particular type of assignment, they do not repeat previous, detrimental behavior; rather, they seek expert advice from a professional educator on how best to improve.

10. Students with superior grades are aware of the teacher's expectations and the school marking system. Academically superior students know and understand what the teacher expects from them; consequently, they ensure that their schoolwork reflects these expectations. They understand the school marking process and how teachers are required to mark student assignments and tests. If a dispute should arise regarding school marks and grades, the students' knowledge of the school system and the marking process allows them to argue successfully for higher marks and grades.

Teacher/Parent Meeting Agenda

(The following form should be completed by the teacher or administrator-in-charge. Section B of this form should be completed prior to meeting with parents and administrators.)

A. Names of individuals in attendance: _____

Chairperson: _____ Meeting requested by _____

Date of Meeting: _____

B. Meeting Agenda (This section is to be completed prior to the meeting):

1. _____
2. _____
3. _____
4. _____
5. _____

C. Meeting Minutes (Note participant's statements as they relate to the above agenda):

1. _____
2. _____
3. _____
4. _____
5. _____

D. Conclusions and Comments:

_____

_____

_____

_____

Course of Action to be taken by Subject Teacher: _____

Course of Action to be taken by Student/Parent: _____

Course of Action to be taken by Principal: _____

Next Meeting Date: _____

Signatures: _____ Date: _____

_____

Request for Re-evaluation of Student Work

The student or parent is to complete this form prior to a formal re-evaluation. (Check the boxes as you complete this form.)

❏ This request is made by _____.

❏ The subject teacher's name is _____.

❏ The course or subject is _____.

❏ The date of my request is made on _____.

❏ The title of the assignment is _____.

❏ Below, clearly state your request:

_____

_____

_____

_____

❏ Below, clearly state why you believe this work should be re-evaluated.
   (State why you believe the original mark is inaccurate.):

_____

_____

_____

_____

_____

_____

_____

❏ If possible, attach to this page a copy of the teacher's original assignment instructions.

❏ If possible, attach to this page a copy of the teacher's stated marking criteria.

I, the undersigned, am asking for the above-mentioned student work to be re-evaluated. The re-evaluation process has been explained to me and I fully understand this process.

_____   _____
Signature of Parent or Student   Date

Confidential Re-evaluation Report

The second evaluator or principal is to check each box to ensure that all steps of the re-marking process have been followed.

❑ The subject teacher has been informed of the request for re-evaluation.

❑ A formal request for re-evaluation has been made by _____.

❑ Student work to be re-evaluated by _____.

❑ The complainant has been informed of all procedures in the re-marking process, and has been told of the possible consequences.

❑ The complainant has submitted a copy of the work to be re-evaluated.

❑ The second marker has received a copy of the student's work to be re-evaluated.

❑ The second marker has received a copy of the teacher's assignment and the marking criteria.

Comments of Second Evaluator:

_____

_____

_____

_____

_____

_____

_____

_____

_____

New Mark: _____

❑ The subject teacher, complainant, and principal have been informed of the second marker's evaluation.

_____   _____
Second Marker   School Principal

_____   _____
Subject Teacher   Student/Parent

Date _____

A Final Thought about Marking and Letter Grades

How does the teacher measure the success of his life? At the end of the day, the only thing that remains is the vain hope that through the din, some student "got it."

This book ends the same way it began—with a quote from a professor. Only this time, it comes from my father, a man who taught his own university course for more than 30 years. When I was at the impressionable age of ten, over a dinner-time conversation regarding some mundane event in my elementary school life, he remarked to me that "school teaching seems like a sad job." Sad, he clarified, because the children grow up, move on, and are never seen again by the teacher. But now, as an adult, I suspect he meant more. Every time teachers teach, they reveal a part of themselves. They impart not only knowledge, but their ways of looking at the world. By interacting with students, the teacher hopes to make a small difference in the world and the chance to say, "I contributed, and I had an impact." And yet, really, what does the teacher leave behind? How does a teacher measure the success of his or her life? At the end of the day, the only thing that remains is the vain hope that through the din, some student "got it."

The vast majority of teachers are dedicated professionals who are genuinely concerned with the well-being of their students. They want to see all of their students succeed in school and in their future career paths. They recognize the value of a student's school transcript marks, and that these marks can mean the difference between success and failure in that student's endeavors. This can place a teacher in a somewhat awkward role, as the teacher must be careful to mediate a thin line between comrade and authoritarian—step too far over the line in one direction and the teacher loses control and the respect of students; too far the other way, and the teacher is perceived as a heartless tyrant. Yet always, the teacher's expressed concern must be for the academic welfare of the student. When student evaluation leads to interpersonal conflict, as it sometimes does, it is to the teacher's advantage to take the high ground and to express a caring, compassionate, and professional demeanor. It is good politics. It is a part of good teaching. Indeed, every time teachers assign a mark, they are reminded that they may be required to explain, to justify, and to defend their professional marking decisions. The best way for teachers to defend their evaluative decisions is to rely on a marking process that is research-driven, transparent, and universally applied.

Teacher Resource Bibliography

Airasian, Peter W. *Classroom Assessment: Concepts and Applications.* New York, NY: McGraw-Hill, 2001.

Borich, Gary D. *Effective Teaching Methods.* Columbus, OH: Merrill, 1988.

Chatterji, Madhabi. *Designing and Using Tools for Educational Assessment.* Boston, MA: Pearson Education, 2003.

Cotton, Julie. *The Theory of Assessment: An Introduction.* London, UK: Kogan Page, 1995.

Fenwick, Tara and Parsons, Jim. *The Art of Evaluation: A Handbook for Educators and Trainers.* Toronto, ON: Thompson Educational, 2000.

Goodman, Greg S. and Carey, Karen T. *Ubiquitous Assessment: Evaluation Techniques for the New Millenium.* New York, NY: Peter Lang, 2004.

Gronlund, Norman E. *Assessment of Student Achievement* (6th edition). Boston, MA: Allyn and Bacon, 1998.

Hopkins, Charles D. and Antes, Richard L. *Classroom Measurement and Evaluation* (3rd edition). Itasca, IL: F. E. Peacock, 1990.

Hopkins, Kenneth D. *Educational and Psychological Measurement and Evaluation* (8th edition). Boston, MA: Allyn and Bacon, 1998.

Johnson, David W. and Johnson, Roger T. *Meaningful Assessment: A Manageable and Cooperative Process.* Boston, MA: Allyn and Bacon, 2002.

Marzano, Robert J. *Transforming Classroom Grading.* Alexandria, VI: Association for Supervision and Curriculum Development, 2004.

McMillan, James H. *Classroom Assessment: Principles and Practice for Effective Instruction.* Boston, MA: Allyn and Bacon, 2001.

McMillan, James H. *Essential Assessment Concepts for Teachers and Administrators.* Thousand Oaks, CA: Corwin Press, 2001.

Nitko, Anthony J. *Educational Assessment of Students* (2nd edition). Columbus, OH: Merrill, 1996.

Oosterhoff, Albert. *Classroom Applications of Educational Measurment* (3rd edition). Upper Saddle River, NJ: Merrill Prentice Hall, 2001.

Osterlind, Steven J. *Constructing Test Items: Multiple-Choice, Constructed Response, Performance, and Other Formats* (2nd edition). Norwell, MA: Kluwer Academic Publishers, 1998.

Payne, David Allen. *Applied Educational Assessment.* Belmont, CA: Wadsworth, 1997.

Popham, James W. *Classroom Assessment: What Teachers Need to Know* (4th edition). Boston, MA: Pearson Education, 2005.

Popham, James W. *Modern Educational Measurement: Practical Guidelines for Educational Leaders* (3rd edition). Boston, MA: Allyn and Bacon, 2000.

Schumacher, Sally and McMillan, James H. *Research in Education: A Conceptual Introduction.* New York, NY: HarperCollins, 1993.

Smith, J. K., Smith, L. F. and De Lisi, Richard. *Classroom Assessment: Designing Seamless Instruction and Assessment.* Thousand Oaks, CA: Corwin Press, 2001.

Tenbrink, Terry D. *Evaluation: A Practical Guide for Teachers.* New York, NY: McGraw-Hill, 1974.

Wiggins, Grant P. *Assessing Student Performance: Exploring the Purpose and Limits of testing.* San Francisco, CA: Jossey-Bass, 1993.

Wiggins, Grant. *Educative Assessment: Designing Assessments to Inform and Improve Student Performance.* San Francisco, CA: Jossey-Bass, 1998.

Woolfolk, Anita E. *Educational Psychology* (9th edition). Boston, MA: Allyn and Bacon, 2003.

Ysseldyke, Salvia. *Assessment* (7th edition). New York, NY: Houghton Mifflin, 1998.

Index